Steck-Vaughn

English ASAP™

Connecting English to the Workplace

O9-BTO-421

SCANS Consultant

Shirley Brod
Spring Institute for International Studies
Boulder, Colorado

Program Consultants

Judith Dean-Griffin
ESL Teacher
Windham Independent School District
Texas Department of Criminal Justice
Huntsville, Texas

Marilyn K. Spence
Workforce Education Coordinator
Orange Technical Education Centers
Mid-Florida Tech
Orlando, Florida

Brigitte Marshall
English Language Training
for Employment Participation
Albany, California

Dennis Terdy
Director, Community Education
Township High School District 214
Arlington Heights, Illinois

Christine Kay Williams
ESL Specialist
Towson University
Baltimore, Maryland

STECK-VAUGHN
COMPANY

A Division of Harcourt Brace & Company

Acknowledgments

Executive Editor:	Ellen Northcutt
Supervising Editor:	Tim Collins
Assistant Art Director:	Richard Balsam
Interior Design:	Richard Balsam, Jill Klinger, Paul Durick
Electronic Production:	Jill Klinger, Stephanie Stewart, Alan Klemp
Assets Manager:	Margie Foster

Editorial Development: Course Crafters, Inc., Newburyport, Massachusetts

Photo Credits

Alhadeff–p.15b, 15c, 27b, 34-35, 39a, 39b, 39c, 46-47, 51d, 58-59, 63a, 63c, 94-95, 106-107, 114, 118-119; Don Couch Photography–p.75a, 75c, 87a, 87b, 87d, 111d; Jack Demuth–p.3a, 3c, 15d, 27a, 27c, 51b, 52a, 52b, 87c, 99a, 99b, 116; Patrick Dunn–p.27d, 111c; Christine Galida-p.15a, 54, 57, 63b, 65, 111a, 111b, 113; David Omer–p.22-23, 82-83; Park Street–p.10-11, 30, 39d, 51a, 51c, 70-71, 75b, 75d, 99d; Ken Walker–p.3b, 3d, 52c, 73, 99c.

Illustration Credits

Cover: Tim Dove, D Childress

Cindy Aarvig–16, 19; Karl Bailey–24, 28a, 28c-i, 35c, 35e, 91; Richard Balsam–6, 10-12, 14, 31, 33, 34, 35f, 37, 40b, 46, 49b, 95b, 96e-h, 97b, 104; Chris Celusniak–29, 42, 89, 90, 97a; David Griffin–17, 18, 25, 88, 98; Dennis Harms–36, 38; Laura Jackson–28b, 28j, 35a-b, 35d; Chuck Joseph–41, 64, 71, 76, 82-86, 100, 106-109, 112, 118-122; Linda Kelen–66, 96a-d; Michael Krone–5, 53, 68, 69, 92, 93; John Scott–21, 94, 95a; kreativ-design/ Danielle Szabo–3, 15, 22, 23, 26, 27, 39, 40a, 43, 45, 47, 48, 49a, 50, 51, 58, 59, 61, 62, 63, 70, 72, 74, 75, 87, 99, 111; Victoria Vebell–77, 78, 101, 102.

ISBN 0-8172-7952-0

Contents

Introduction to Student Book 2 iv

1 Communication 3
• Take telephone messages • Answer the telephone at work • Make telephone calls
• Find the telephone numbers you need

2 Your Workplace 15
• Get the supplies you need • Organize materials • Maintain supplies and equipment
• Use file systems

3 Technology 27
• Complete a maintenance request • Talk about problems with machines • Read a user's manual

4 Time Management 39
• Understand schedules • Interpret a holiday schedule • Use calendars and planners

5 Customer Service 51
• Respond to requests • Handle special requests • Offer suggestions • Understand customer
service policies

6 Culture of Work 63
• Follow rules • Make compromises • Understand company goals • Get along with others

7 Finances 75
• Understand a paycheck • Report mistakes in your paycheck • Understand information about
Social Security • Understand a W-2 form

8 Health and Safety 87
• Understand safety instructions • Follow safety instructions • Complete an accident report
• Report unsafe situations

9 Working with People 99
• Understand an agenda • Prepare for a meeting • Ask questions in a meeting
• Make meetings work for you

10 Career Development 111
• Look for a job • Interview for a job • Understand hiring decisions • Complete a job application

Listening Transcript 123

Vocabulary 132

Irregular Verbs 133

Introduction to Student Book 2

About SCANS, the Workforce, and *English ASAP: Connecting English to the Workplace*

SCANS and the Workforce

The Secretary's Commission on Achieving Necessary Skills (SCANS) was established by the U.S. Department of Labor in 1990. Its mission was to study the demands of workplace environments and determine whether people entering the workforce are capable of meeting those demands. The commission identified skills for employment, suggested ways for assessing proficiency, and devised strategies to implement the identified skills. The commission's first report, entitled *What Work Requires of Schools—SCANS Report for America 2000,* was published in June 1991. The report is designed for use by educators (curriculum developers, job counselors, training directors, and teachers) to prepare the modern workforce for the workplace with viable, up-to-date skills.

The report identified two types of skills: Competencies and Foundations. There are five SCANS Competencies: (1) Resources, (2) Interpersonal, (3) Information, (4) Systems, and (5) Technology. There are three parts contained in SCANS Foundations: (1) Basic Skills (including reading, writing, arithmetic, mathematics, listening, and speaking); (2) Thinking Skills (including creative thinking, decision making, problem solving, seeing things in the mind's eye, knowing how to learn, and reasoning); and (3) Personal Qualities (including responsibility, self-esteem, sociability, self-management, and integrity/honesty).

Steck-Vaughn's *English ASAP: Connecting English to the Workplace*

English ASAP is a complete SCANS-based, four-skills program for teaching ESL and SCANS skills to adults and young adults. *English ASAP* follows a work skills-based syllabus that is compatible with the CASAS and MELT competencies. *English ASAP* has these components:

Student Books

The Student Books are designed to allow from 125 to 235 hours of instruction. Each Student Book contains 10 units of SCANS-based instruction. A Listening Transcript of material appearing on the Audiocassettes and a Vocabulary list, organized by unit, of core workforce-based words and phrases appear at the back of each Student Book. Because unit topics carry over from level to level, *English ASAP* is ideal for multi-level classes.

The *On Your Job* symbol appears on the Student Book page each time learners apply a work skill to their own jobs or career interests.

An abundance of tips throughout each unit provides information and strategies that learners can use to be more effective workers and language learners.

Teacher's Editions

Teacher's Editions provide reduced Student Book pages with answers inserted and wraparound teacher notes that give detailed suggestions on how to present each page of the Student Book in class. Teacher's Editions 1 and 2 also provide blackline masters to reinforce the grammar in each unit. The Literacy Level Teacher's Edition contains blackline masters that provide practice with many basic literacy skills. The complete Listening Transcript, Vocabulary, charts for tracking individual and class success, and a Certificate of Completion appear at the back of each Teacher's Edition.

Workbooks

The Workbooks, starting at Level 1, provide reinforcement for each section of the Student Books.

Audiocassettes

The Audiocassettes contain all the dialogs and listening activities in the Student Books.

 This symbol appears on the Student Book page and corresponding Teacher's Edition page each time material for that page is recorded on the Audiocassettes. A Listening Transcript of all material recorded on the tapes but not appearing directly on the Student Book pages is at the back of each Student Book and Teacher's Edition.

Workforce Writing Dictionary

Steck-Vaughn's *Workforce Writing Dictionary*, is a 96-page custom dictionary that allows learners to create a personalized, alphabetical list of the key words and phrases they need to know for their jobs. Each letter of the alphabet is allocated two to four pages for learners to record the language they need. In addition, each letter is illustrated with several workforce-related words.

Placement Tests

The Placement Tests, Form A and Form B, can be used as entry and exit tests and to assist in placing learners in the appropriate level of *English ASAP.*

Placement

In addition to the Placement Tests, the following table indicates placement based on the CASAS and new MELT student performance level standards.

Placement

New MELT SPL	CASAS Achievement Score	English ASAP
0–1	179 or under	Literacy
2–3	180–200	Level 1
4–5	201–220	Level 2

About Student Book 2

Organization of a Unit

Each twelve-page unit contains these nine sections: Unit Opener, Getting Started, Talk About It, Keep Talking, Listening, Grammar, Reading and Writing, Extension, and Performance Check.

Unit Opener

Each Unit Opener includes photos and several related, work-focused questions. The photos and questions activate learners' prior knowledge by getting them to think and talk about the unit topic. The **Performance Preview**, which gives an overview of all the skills in the unit, helps teachers set goals and purposes for the unit. Optionally, teachers may want to examine the Performance Preview with learners before they begin the unit.

Getting Started

An initial **Team Work** activity presents key work skills, concepts, and language introduced in the unit. It consists of active critical thinking and peer teaching to activate the use of the new language and to preview the content of the unit. A **Partner Work** or **Practice the**

To the Teacher

Dialog activity encourages learners to use the new language in communicative ways. A culminating class or group **Survey** encourages learners to relate the new language to themselves and their workplaces or career interests.

Talk About It

This page provides opportunities for spoken communication. **Practice the Dialog** provides a model for conversation. **Partner Work** presents a personalized **On Your Job** activity that allows learners to use the model in Practice the Dialog to talk about their own workplace experiences.

The **Useful Language** box contains related words, phrases, and expressions for learners to use as they complete Partner Work.

The **ASAP Project** is a long-term project learners complete over the course of the unit. Learners create items such as a class telephone roster, a workplace safety booklet, and a file of tax and payroll forms they can use outside of the classroom.

Keep Talking

The Keep Talking page contains additional conversation models and speaking tasks. It also includes the **Personal Dictionary** feature. This feature allows learners to record the language relevant to the unit topic that they need to do their jobs. Because each learner's job is different, this personalized resource enables learners to focus on the language that is most useful to them. In addition, learners can use this feature in conjunction with Steck-Vaughn's *Workforce Writing Dictionary* to create a completely customized lexicon of key words and phrases they need to know.

Listening

The Listening page develops SCANS-based listening skills. Activities include listening to and understanding customer requests, employee performance reviews, safety instructions, and workplace meetings.

All the activities develop the skill of **focused listening.** Learners learn to recognize the information they need and to listen selectively for only that information. They do not have to understand every word; rather, they have to filter out everything except the relevant information. This essential skill is used by native speakers of all languages.

Many of the activities involve **multi-task listening.** In these activities, called **Listen Again** and **Listen Once More**, learners listen to the same selection several times and complete a different task each time. First they might listen for the main idea. They might listen again for specific information. They might listen a third time in order to draw conclusions or make inferences.

Culminating discussion questions allow learners to relate the information they have heard to their own needs and interests.

A complete Listening Transcript for all dialogs recorded on the Audiocassettes but not on the Student Book pages is at the back of the Student Book and Teacher's Edition. All the selections are recorded on the Audiocassettes.

Grammar

Grammar, a two-page spread, presents key grammatical structures that complement the unit competencies. Language boxes show the new language in a clear, simple format that allows learners to make generalizations about the new language. Oral and written exercises provide contextualized reinforcement relevant to the workplace.

Reading and Writing

Reading selections, such as help wanted ads, meeting agendas, and company rules, focus on items learners encounter at work. Exercises and discussion questions develop reading skills and help learners relate the content of the selections to their workplaces or career interests.

The writing tasks, often related to the reading selection, help learners develop writing skills, such as completing job applications, filling out a Social Security form and completing a personal calendar/planner.

Extension

The Extension page enriches the previous instruction. As in other sections, realia is used extensively. Oral and written exercises help learners master the additional skills, language, and concepts, and relate them to their workplaces and career interests.

CultureNotes **Culture Notes**, a feature that appears on each Extension page, sparks lively, engaging discussion. Topics include holidays across cultures, the importance of customer service, and using active listening during meetings.

Performance Check

The two-page Performance Check allows teachers and learners to track learners' progress and to meet the learner verification needs of schools, companies, or programs. All work skills are tested in the same manner they are presented in the units; so, formats are familiar and non-threatening, and success is built in. The **Performance Review** at the end of each test alerts teachers and learners to the work skills that are being evaluated. The check-off boxes allow learners to track their success and gain a sense of accomplishment and satisfaction. Finally, a culminating discussion allows learners to relate their new skills to their development as effective workers.

Teaching Techniques

Make Your Classroom Mirror the Workplace

Help learners develop workplace skills by setting up your classroom to mirror a workplace. Use any of these suggestions.

◆ Establish policies on lateness and absence similar to those a business might have.

◆ Provide learners with a daily agenda of the activities they will complete that day, including partner work and small group assignments. Go over the agenda with learners at the beginning and end of class.

◆ With learner input, establish a list of goals for the class. Goals can include speaking, reading, and writing English every day; using effective teamwork skills; or learning ten new vocabulary words each day. Go over the goals with learners at regular intervals.

◆ Assign students regular jobs and responsibilities, such as arranging the chairs in a circle, setting up the overhead projector, or making copies for the class.

Presenting a Unit Opener

The unit opener sets the stage for the unit. Use the photos and questions to encourage learners to:

◆ Speculate about what the unit might cover.

◆ Activate prior knowledge.

◆ Relate what they see in the photos to their own work environments.

Peer Teaching

Because each adult learner brings rich life experience to the classroom, *English ASAP* is designed to help you use each learner's expertise as a resource for peer teaching.

Here are some practical strategies for peer teaching:

◆ Have learners work in pairs/small groups to clarify new language concepts for each other.

◆ If a learner possesses a particular work skill, appoint that learner as "class consultant" in that area and have learners direct queries to that individual.

To the Teacher

◆ Set up a reference area in a corner of your classroom. Include dictionaries, career books, and other books your learners will find useful.

Partner Work and Team Work

The abundance of Partner Work and Team Work activities in *English ASAP* serves the dual purposes of developing learners' communicative competence and providing learners with experience using key SCANS interpersonal skills, such as working in teams, teaching others, leading, negotiating, and working well with people from culturally diverse backgrounds. To take full advantage of these activities, follow these suggestions.

◆ Whenever learners work in groups, appoint, or have students select, a leader.

◆ Use multiple groupings. Have learners work with different partners and teams, just as workers do in the workplace. For different activities, you might group learners according to language ability, skill, or learner interest.

◆ Make sure learners understand that everyone on the team is responsible for the team's work.

◆ At the end of each activity, have teams report the results to the class.

◆ Discuss with learners their teamwork skills and talk about ways teams can work together effectively. Learners can discuss how to clarify roles and responsibilities, resolve disagreements effectively, communicate openly, and make decisions together.

Purpose Statement

Each page after the unit opener begins with a brief purpose statement that summarizes the work skills presented on that page. When learners first begin working on a page, focus their attention on the purpose statement and help them read it. Ask them what the page will

be about. Discuss with the class why the skill is important. Ask learners to talk about their prior knowledge of the skill. Finally, show learners how using the skill will help them become more effective on their jobs.

Survey

The **Survey** on each **Getting Started** page helps learners relate the new language and skills to their own lives. Before learners begin the activity, help them create questions they'll need to ask. Assist them in deciding how they'll record their answers. You may need to model taking notes, using tally marks, and other simple ways to record information. Assist learners in setting a time limit before they begin. Remember to allow learners to move about the room as they complete the activity.

Many Survey results can be summarized in a bar graph or pie chart.

◆ A bar graph uses bars to represent numbers. Bar graphs have two scales, a vertical scale and a horizontal scale. For example, to graph the number of learners who get paid by check versus those paid by direct deposit, the vertical scale can represent numbers of students, such as 2, 4, 6, 8, etc. The horizontal scale can consist of two bars. One bar represents the number of learners paid by check. The other bar represents the number of learners paid by direct deposit. The two bars can be different colors to set them apart. Bars should be the same width.

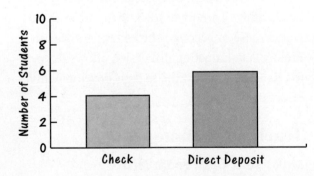

- A pie chart shows the parts that make up a whole set of facts. Each part of the pie is a percentage of the whole. For example, a pie chart might show 40% of learners are paid by check and 60% are paid by direct deposit.

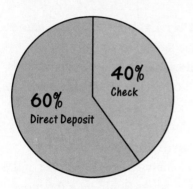

Presenting a Dialog

To present a dialog, follow these suggested steps:

- Play the tape or say the dialog aloud two or more times. Ask one or two simple questions to make sure learners understand.

- Say the dialog aloud line-by-line for learners to repeat chorally, by rows, and then individually.

- Have learners say or read the dialog together in pairs.

- Have several pairs say or read the dialog aloud for the class.

Presenting the Personal Dictionary

The Personal Dictionary enables learners to focus on the vocabulary in each unit that is relevant to their particular jobs. To use this feature, have learners work in teams to brainstorm vocabulary words they might put in their dictionaries. Have team reporters share their ideas with the class. Then allow learners a few minutes to add to their dictionaries. Remind students to continue adding words throughout the unit.

For further vocabulary development, learners can enter the words from their Personal Dictionary into their *Workforce Writing Dictionaries.*

To the Teacher

Presenting a Listening Activity

Use any of these suggestions:

- To activate learners' prior knowledge, have them look at the illustrations, if any, and say as much as they can about them. Encourage them to make inferences about the content of the listening selection.

- Have learners read the directions. To encourage them to focus their listening, have them read the questions before they listen so that they know exactly what to listen for.

- Play the tape or read the Listening Transcript aloud as learners complete the activity. Rewind the tape and play it again as necessary.

- Help learners check their work.

In multi-task listening, remind learners that they will listen to the same passage several times and answer different questions each time. After learners complete a section, have them check their own or each others' work before you rewind the tape and proceed to the next questions.

Presenting a Tip

A variety of tips throughout each unit present valuable advice on how to be a successful employee and/or language learner. To present a tip, help learners read the tip. Discuss it with them. Ask them how it will help them. For certain tips, such as those in which learners make lists, you may want to allow learners time to start the activity.

Presenting a Discussion

English ASAP provides a variety of whole-class and team discussions. Always encourage students to state their ideas and respond appropriately to other learners' comments. At the end of each discussion, have team reporters summarize their team's ideas and/or help the class come to a consensus about the topic.

Prereading

To help learners read the selections with ease and success, establish a purpose for reading and call on learners' prior knowledge to make inferences about the reading. Use any of these techniques:

◆ Have learners look over and describe any photographs, realia, and/or illustrations. Ask them to use the illustrations to say what they think the selection might be about.

◆ Have learners read the title and any heads or sub-heads. Ask them what kind of information they think is in the selection and how it might be organized. Ask them where they might encounter such information outside of class and why they would want to read it.

◆ To help learners focus their reading, have them review the comprehension activities before they read the selection. Ask them what kind of information they think they will find out when they read. Restate their ideas and/or write them on the board in acceptable English.

◆ Remind learners that they do not have to know all the words in order to understand the selection.

Evaluation

To use the Performance Check pages successfully, follow these suggested procedures:
Before and during each evaluation, create a relaxed, affirming atmosphere. Chat with the learners for a few minutes and review the material. When you and the learners are ready, have learners read the directions and look over each exercise before they complete it. If at any time you sense that learners are becoming frustrated, stop to provide additional review. Resume when learners are ready. The evaluation formats follow two basic patterns:

1. **Speaking** competencies are checked in the format used to present them in the unit. Have learners read the instructions. Make sure learners know what to do. Then have learners complete the evaluation in one of these ways:

Self- and Peer Evaluation: Have learners complete the spoken activity in pairs. Learners in each pair evaluate themselves and/or each other and report the results to you.

Teacher/Pair Evaluation: Have pairs complete the activity as you observe and evaluate their work. Begin with the most proficient learners. As other learners who are ready to be evaluated wait, have them practice in pairs. Learners who complete the evaluation successfully can peer-teach those who are waiting or those who need additional review.

Teacher/Individual Evaluation: Have individuals complete the activity with you as their partner. Follow the procedures in Teacher/Pair Evaluation.

2. **Listening, reading,** and **writing** competencies are also all checked in the same format used to present them in the unit. When learners are ready to begin, have them read the instructions. Demonstrate the first item and have learners complete the activity. In Listening activities, play the tape or read the listening transcript aloud two or more times. Then have learners check their work. Provide any review needed, and have learners try the activity again.

When learners demonstrate mastery of a skill to your satisfaction, have them record their success by checking the appropriate box in the Performance Review. The Teacher's Edition also contains charts for you to reproduce to keep track of individual and class progress.

Steck-Vaughn

English ASAP™

Connecting English to the Workplace

Communication

What do you think?

Look at the pictures.

What are the people doing?

What do you say when you answer the telephone?

Performance Preview

Can you...

☐ 1. take telephone messages?

☐ 2. answer the telephone at work?

☐ 3. make telephone calls?

☐ 4. find the telephone numbers you need?

TEAM WORK

Work with a team. Match the caller and the person answering the telephone. Then say the telephone conversations aloud.

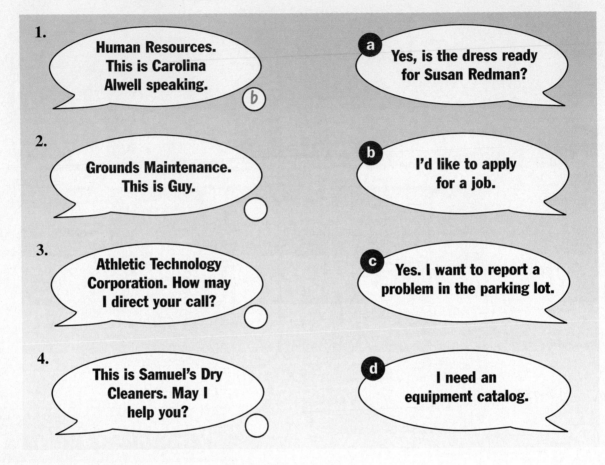

1. Human Resources. This is Carolina Alwell speaking. (b)

    a Yes, is the dress ready for Susan Redman?

2. Grounds Maintenance. This is Guy. ( )

    b I'd like to apply for a job.

3. Athletic Technology Corporation. How may I direct your call? ( )

    c Yes. I want to report a problem in the parking lot.

4. This is Samuel's Dry Cleaners. May I help you? ( )

    d I need an equipment catalog.

PARTNER WORK

Practice the dialog. Then use the dialog to make calls for your job.

A Shipping department. This is Lou.

B This is Paul Smith. May I please speak to the manager?

SURVEY

How do you answer the telephone at work? Write down what you say. Compare your answers with your classmates' answers. What is the most common way to answer the telephone?

PRACTICE THE DIALOG

A This is Ana Smith. May I help you?

B Ana, it's Marta. Do you know Ruby Lee's number? It's not on my telephone roster or in my Rolodex.

A Ruby Lee's number? I have it. It's 555-7913.

B 555-7913. Thanks, Ana. Bye.

PARTNER WORK

Take turns asking for telephone numbers in Ana's Rolodex. Use the dialog and Useful Language above.

Useful Language

I'm looking for Ruby's telephone number.

I can look it up for you.

Tip Carry important telephone numbers in your purse or wallet.

ASAP
PROJECT

Make a class telephone roster. Team 1 puts names in alphabetical order. Team 2 gets the telephone numbers. Team 3 gets the best times for people to call. Complete this project as you work through this unit.

 **Answering telephone calls**

 PRACTICE THE DIALOG

A Thanks for calling Pizza House. Can I take your order?

B Yes, I'd like a small pizza with mushrooms.

A What's your name and address?

B Carmen Diaz. D-I-A-Z. I'm at 16 Bank Street.

A A small pizza with mushrooms for Diaz at 16 Bank Street. We'll be there in thirty minutes.

B Great! Thanks.

Pizza Size (check one)

✓ small ___ medium ___ large

Toppings (check one or more)

___ cheese ___ green peppers ___ sausage

✓ mushrooms ___ ham ___ pepperoni

Caller's Name (write in) _Carmen Diaz_

Caller's Address (write in) _16 Bank St._

PARTNER WORK

Take turns ordering a pizza. Write your partner's order on the form. Write the name and address. Use the dialog and Useful Language.

Pizza Size (check one)

___ small ___ medium ___ large

Toppings (check one or more)

___ cheese ___ green peppers ___ sausage

___ mushrooms ___ ham ___ pepperoni

Caller's Name (write in) _____

Caller's Address (write in) _____

Useful Language

Thanks for calling . . .

Would you like . . . ?

How do you spell that?

Personal Dictionary ▸ Using the Telephone

Write the words and phrases that you need to know.

_____

_____

_____

6 Unit 1

 **Listening** Understanding telephone messages

 LISTEN AND CIRCLE

Circle the name of the caller.

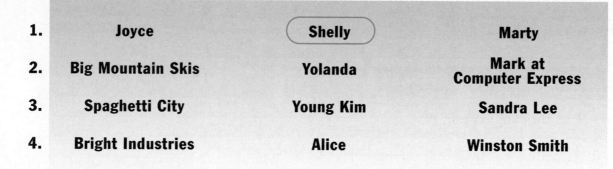

1.	Joyce	(Shelly)	Marty
2.	Big Mountain Skis	Yolanda	Mark at Computer Express
3.	Spaghetti City	Young Kim	Sandra Lee
4.	Bright Industries	Alice	Winston Smith

 LISTEN AGAIN

Write the caller's telephone number or extension.

1. _____3317_____

2. _____

3. _____

4. _____

 When someone tells you his or her name and you don't understand, ask for the spelling:

Could you spell that, please?

 LISTEN ONCE MORE

Circle the reason for each call.

1. (a.) The caller needs two staplers today.

   b. The caller wants to know if Shelly is in the supply room.

2. a. The caller wants to sell Yolanda a computer.

   b. The caller wants to tell Yolanda that the office computer is ready.

3. a. The caller wants to call in sick.

   b. The caller wants a job.

4. a. The caller wants to tell Alice that he will pay the invoice by Friday.

   b. The caller wants to tell Alice that he can't find the invoice.

Grammar — Learning the language you need

A. Study the Examples

I'm	in the hall.
He's	
She's	
It's	

You're	in the hall.
We're	
They're	

Tip Use "you" for only one person. Use "you" for two or more people, too.

COMPLETE THE SENTENCES

Use the language in A.

1. I am the supervisor. I __'m__ in my office.

2. The workers are in the factory. They _____ at a team meeting.

3. My boss is named Martina. She _____ at her desk.

4. Carlos, Margo, and I work together. We _____ a good team.

5. My extension is new. It _____ 2287.

6. You and Jim work hard. You _____ always busy.

7. Mark makes a lot of decisions. He _____ very busy.

B. Study the Examples

I	answer the telephone.
We	
You	
They	

He	answers the telephone.
She	
It	

COMPLETE THE SENTENCES

1. I __take__ (take) messages.

2. He _____ (open) the mail.

3. We _____ (ask) questions.

4. They _____ (help) customers.

 **PARTNER WORK**

Use the language in B. Talk about the work you do.

C. Study the Examples

I We You They	have a message.

He She It	has a message.

COMPLETE THE SENTENCES

Use the words from C.

1. My company __has__ an opening for a shipping clerk.

2. My coworkers and I _____ team meetings on Mondays.

3. The company _____ a pick-up truck.

 TEAM WORK

What machines does your workplace have? Make a list.
Share your list with the class.

Tim's workplace has six cash registers.

D. Study the Examples

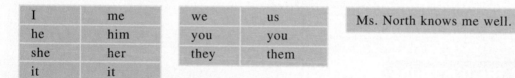

I	me
he	him
she	her
it	it

we	us
you	you
they	them

Ms. North knows me well.

COMPLETE THE DIALOG

A Do you know Margo Wong?

B Yes. I know __her__ (**them/her**).

A Do you know her telephone number?

B Yes, I have _____ (**us/it**) in my Rolodex.

A Good, she always forgets to give it to _____ (**it/me**).

B OK, I'll write _____ (**it/him**) down for you.

 TEAM WORK

Who do you call at work? Why do you call them?
Make a list.

Unit 1

Reading and Writing

READ THE TELEPHONE MESSAGE

For _Leonard_

Date _April 3_ Time _2:30_

While You Were Out

From _Ruby Lee_

From _Advertising Department_

Phone _x3439_

TELEPHONED	X	CAME TO SEE YOU	
PLEASE CALL	X	WILL CALL AGAIN	

MESSAGE _She needs a parking sticker._

_____

_____

SIGNED _____

Tip When you get a phone message, it's a good idea to call back right away.

ANSWER THE QUESTIONS

1. Who's the message for? _____Leonard_____

2. Who called? _____

3. What time did she call? _____

4. What does she need? _____

5. What's her extension? _____

DISCUSSION

What do you think Leonard will do? Why?

Use the dialog to complete the phone message. Use today's date and the time now.

A Hello. Sales Office.

B Hi. Is Pedro Martinez in?

A Pedro's out of the office. This is David Salinas. Can I help you?

B Yes. This is Li Tran in Customer Service. I need ten catalogs. Can you tell Pedro to call me?

A Sure. What's your extension?

B It's 3317.

A OK. I'll tell Pedro to call you at extension 3317.

For _____

Date _____ Time _____

While You Were Out

From _____

From _____

Phone _____

TELEPHONED		CAME TO SEE YOU	
PLEASE CALL		WILL CALL AGAIN	

MESSAGE _____

_____

_____

_____

SIGNED _____

Tip When you take a phone message, repeat the caller's phone number.

Was that 555-4801?

DISCUSSION

Work with a team. Talk about the people you need to call.
Do you leave messages? What is a good time to call people?
Share your ideas with the class.

READ AMADO'S LIST

Read Amado's to-do list. Look at the business cards. Write the name and telephone number of each person Amado needs to call.

To Do

6 dozen light bulbs   *Nina Kim, 555-7889*

Advertisement for job opening

Van rental for company picnic

Fix computer

Easy Transport
Fu Chan
Rental Department
555-0901 • Fax 555-0909

Northern Lights
Lighting your world for over 40 years.
Sales Representative
Nina Kim
555-7889

The Daily Tribune
Advertising Representative
Manuel Aznar
1314 Silver Lane, Milton, CA 92290
555-9900 Extension 22

Garcia Computer Repair
555-3221
Marco Garcia
Technician

ANSWER THE QUESTIONS

1. Which department does Fu Chan work in? _the rental department_

2. Who's Nina Kim's employer? _____

3. What's Manuel Aznar's extension? _____

4. What's Marco Garcia's job? _____

CultureNotes

It's easy to dial a wrong number. What do you do when this happens? What do you say?

Performance Check

Complete the activities. Go over your work with a partner or your teacher. Then complete the Performance Review on page 14.

SKILL 1	**TAKE TELEPHONE MESSAGES**

Listen to the telephone calls. Who's calling? Circle the letter.

1. **a.** Martin Valdez

   b. John Drummond

2. **a.** Ms. Mars

   b. Cindy Grey

Listen again. What's the message? Circle the letter.

1. **a.** Call back.

   b. Meet him at 4:00.

2. **a.** The meeting will be at 4:30.

   b. She needs to cancel the meeting.

SKILL 2	**ANSWER TELEPHONE CALLS AT WORK**

You're answering the telephone at Lee's Chinese Restaurant. What do you say? Work with a partner or with your teacher.

SKILL 3	**MAKE TELEPHONE CALLS**

You're ordering a sandwich from The Lunch Stop. What do you say? Work with a partner or with your teacher.

Write the correct telephone extension next to the name.

Landry, Bill . . . . Ext. 7790
Maintenance Department . . . . Ext. 7789
Research and Development . . . Ext. 7870
Santiago, Ernesto . . . . Ext. 9547
Security Department . . . . Ext. 9077

Ernesto Santiago _____

Security Department _____

Research and Development _____

Bill Landry _____

Performance Review

I can...

☐ **1.** take telephone messages.

☐ **2.** answer the telephone at work.

☐ **3.** make telephone calls.

☐ **4.** find the telephone numbers I need.

DISCUSSION

Work with a team. How will your new skills help you?
Make a list. Share your list with the class.

What do you think?

Look at the pictures.

What supplies and equipment do the people use?

What do you do when you need supplies at work?

Performance Preview

Can you...

☐ 1. get the supplies you need?

☐ 2. organize materials?

☐ 3. maintain supplies and equipment?

☐ 4. use file systems?

Getting Started

Talking about work supplies

TEAM WORK

Match the word with the picture. Share your answers with the class.

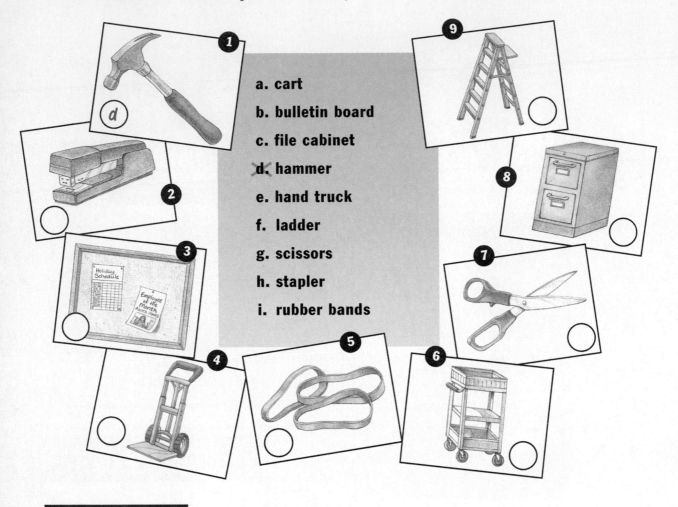

a. cart

b. bulletin board

c. file cabinet

~~d.~~ hammer

e. hand truck

f. ladder

g. scissors

h. stapler

i. rubber bands

PARTNER WORK

Look at the supplies. Student A asks questions. Student B answers.

A Is there a hammer?

B Yes, there is.

A Is there a lawn mower?

B No, there isn't.

 SURVEY

Work with a team. Write a list of five supplies you use at work. Find out how many teammates use the same ones. Which supplies do all of you use? Report your findings to the class.

Unit 2

Getting supplies

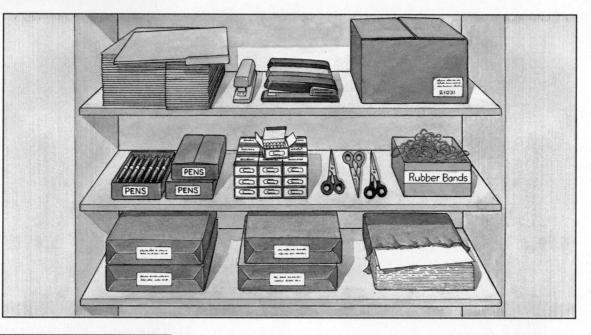

PRACTICE THE DIALOG

A Excuse me. Where's the paper?

B It's on the bottom shelf.

A Where are the rubber bands?

B They're on the middle shelf.

A On the middle shelf?

B Yes, that's right.

A OK, thanks.

Useful Language

I need a . . .

I need some . . .

top	paper clips
middle	pen
bottom	file folder

a box of . . .

a roll of . . .

PARTNER WORK

You and your partner are getting supplies for your work areas.
Talk about the supplies you need. Use the dialog and the
Useful Language above.

ASAP
PROJECT

Choose a shelf in a supply room at your workplace or school and take inventory.
Count all of the supplies. Make a list of the amount of each supply.
Complete this project as you work through this unit.

PARTNER WORK

You work at Handy Copy. Look at two work stations. What is missing from work station 2? Make a list of supplies for work station 2.

 PRACTICE THE DIALOG

Talk about work station 2.
Student A asks for supplies.
Student B answers.

A Work station 2 needs some tape.

B How many rolls should I put out?

A Only one.

B OK.

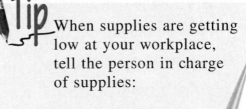

Tip When supplies are getting low at your workplace, tell the person in charge of supplies:

We need some pencils.

Personal Dictionary Supplies

Write the words and phrases that you need to know.

_____

_____

_____

LISTEN AND MATCH

Match the item with its location.

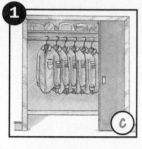 **1** c

 **2** A-B

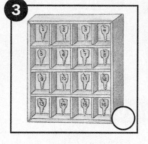 **3**

 **4** PAINT NT NT

 a

 b

 c SUPPLY ROOM

 d A-B C-E F-G H-J K-L M-N O-P Q-R S T U-W X-Z

LISTEN AGAIN

Write the way the next item is organized.

date	letter	number	~~size~~

1. shirts _____ *size*

2. files _____

3. keys _____

4. paint _____

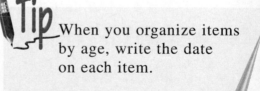

Tip When you organize items by age, write the date on each item.

DISCUSSION

Are the items in Listen Again organized? Are they organized well? Why?
Think about other things you need to organize at home, work, or school.
How do you organize addresses and telephone numbers? money? food?
things in a supply room? Share your ideas with the class.

Grammar — Learning the language you need

A. Study the Examples

Is	there	a bulletin board?
Are		staples in the stapler?

Yes, there	is.		No, there	isn't.
	are.			aren't.

COMPLETE THE DIALOG

A I need to make a personal call.
Is there a telephone in the break room?

B Yes, _____there is_____.

A Great. _____ a calendar in the break room?

B No, _____.

A _____ phone books?

B No, _____. Phone books are in the front office.

A Thanks for your help.

B. Study the Examples

Do you need any	file folders?
	paper?

Yes, I need some.		No, I don't need any.

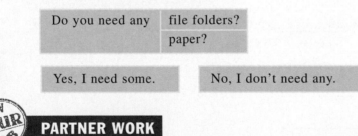

PARTNER WORK

Talk about supplies you need for your jobs.

A Do you need any paper clips?

B No, I don't need any.

C. Study the Examples

There's a ladder	against	the truck.
	behind	
	inside	
	on top of	
	under	
	on	
	over	

COMPLETE THE SENTENCES

Look at the picture. Use the words in C.

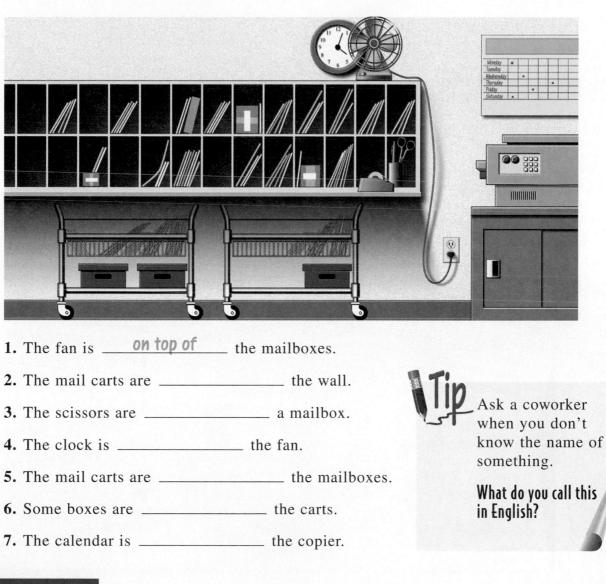

1. The fan is ____on top of____ the mailboxes.

2. The mail carts are _____ the wall.

3. The scissors are _____ a mailbox.

4. The clock is _____ the fan.

5. The mail carts are _____ the mailboxes.

6. Some boxes are _____ the carts.

7. The calendar is _____ the copier.

Tip

Ask a coworker when you don't know the name of something.

What do you call this in English?

TEAM WORK

Take turns describing your classroom or rooms at your workplace. Use the language in C.

Unit 2

21

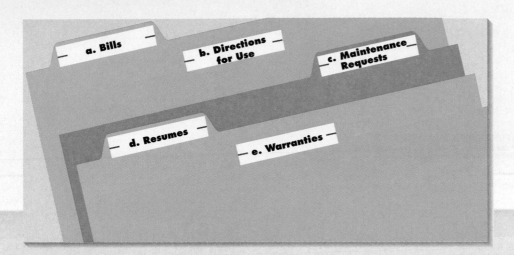

NAME THE FILE

Look at Al's files. What does he keep in each file? Share your ideas with the class.

TEAM WORK

Work with a team. Where would you file Al's papers?
Write the letter of the file.

Maintenance Request (C)

Date: January 26, 1999
Location: Front Door, Main Lobby
Problem: loose door handle
Fix immediately!

Directions for Use
Crafter Electric Paint Sprayer

Invoice

Sunshine Flowers
TO: Al Torres, Costless Sales Co.
DATE: January 27, 1999

Owner's Manual
Worth Electric Pencil Sharpener
Model 3100

User's Guide

Resume

Alex Blanco
1776 Church Street N.E.
Washington, D.C. 20035
(202) 555-7895

Objective
To work in gardening or ground maintenance.

Education
South Guadalupe

Warranty

Crafter Electric Paint Sprayer

TEAM WORK

Your team is organizing your workplace or classroom. Think of papers that you need to organize. How will you organize the papers? By letter of the alphabet? By number? By date? By another method? Write names on the file folders. Share them with your classmates.

Useful Language

Let's put this . . .

This belongs in the . . . file.

Discussion

Did you ever lose an important paper? What did you do?
Can a filing system help you avoid these problems? How?

ON YOUR JOB

MAKE FILES

What files do you need in your workplace, school, or home?
Write a list of file names.

PARTNER WORK

What steps do you take to maintain these tools and supplies?
Match the step with the tool or supply. Can you think of any
other steps?

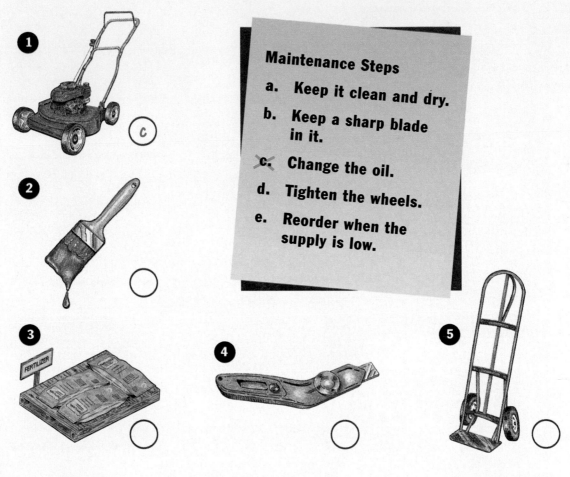

1 ○ c

Maintenance Steps

a. Keep it clean and dry.

b. Keep a sharp blade in it.

~~c.~~ Change the oil.

d. Tighten the wheels.

e. Reorder when the supply is low.

2 ○

3 FERTILIZER ○

4 ○

5 ○

 **PARTNER WORK**

Talk about how you maintain tools and supplies at your workplace.
Share your ideas with the class.

 *CultureNotes*

You see an employee taking a lot of company supplies home.
What do you do? Why?

Complete the activities. Go over your work with a partner or your teacher. Then complete the Performance Review on page 26.

SKILL 1 **GET THE SUPPLIES I NEED**

You are stocking your workplace with supplies. Tell your partner or teacher what supplies you need.

SKILL 2 **ORGANIZE MATERIALS**

How are the things organized? Circle the answer.

1. size   letter of the alphabet

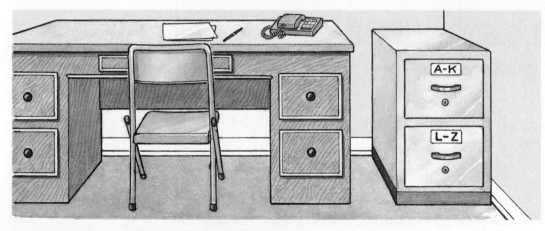

2. date   letter of the alphabet

SKILL 3 **MAINTAIN SUPPLIES AND EQUIPMENT**

What supplies and equipment do you use at your workplace or school? How do you maintain them? Tell your partner or teacher.

Unit 2   25

Read the file names. Read the papers. Where would you file the papers?
Write the letter of the file.

Performance Review

I can...

☐ **1.** get the supplies I need.

☐ **2.** organize materials.

☐ **3.** maintain supplies and equipment.

☐ **4.** use file systems.

DISCUSSION

Work with a team. How will your new skills help you? Make a list.
Share your list with the class.

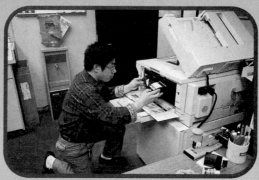

What do you think?

Look at the pictures.

What machines and tools are they using?

What are they doing to take care of the machines and tools?

Performance Preview

Can you...

☐ 1. complete a maintenance request?

☐ 2. talk about problems with machines?

☐ 3. read a user's manual?

Getting Started

Talking about machines at work

TEAM WORK

Match the machine with the object.

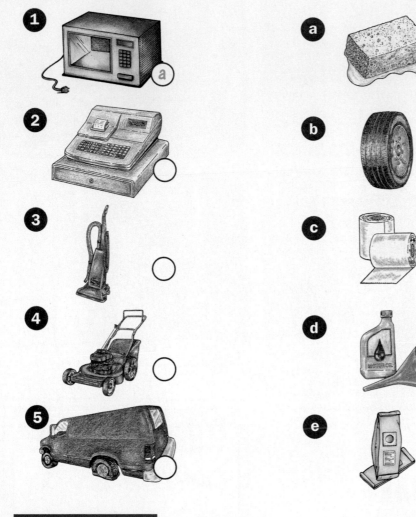

PARTNER WORK

Ask and answer questions about the pictures.
Use the dialog and Useful Language.

A Do you know how to put tape in the
cash register?

B Yes, I do.

Useful Language

put . . . in	clean
change	wash

 **SURVEY**

In a team, list some machines at your workplace. Then write problems
with each machine. Share your list with the class.

28

Unit 3

PRACTICE THE DIALOG

A The vacuum cleaner is broken.

B Did you ask Diane for help?
She can usually fix it.

A Yes, I did. She told me to take it to the
maintenance department.

B Good. Tell the maintenance department we
need the vacuum cleaner repaired today.

PARTNER WORK

Talk about the problems with the machines in the picture. Figure out solutions.
Use the dialog and Useful Language above.

Useful Language

Can you help me with . . .

The coffee maker
isn't working/is leaking/
is out of order.

You need to fill out a
maintenance request.

You should call a plumber/
electrician.

ASAP
PROJECT

As a team, make a user's manual for a machine. Choose a machine you all use.
Write instructions for the machine. Include a drawing. List common problems
with the machine. Tell what to do to fix the problem. Complete this project as
you work through this unit.

Keep Talking Taking care of machines

PARTNER WORK

Circle the pictures that show the right way to care for machines.

PRACTICE THE DIALOG

Talk about the machines above.
Then talk about other machines.

A Don't put your coffee cup on the computer.

B Why?

A You might spill it.

B That's a good point. Thanks.

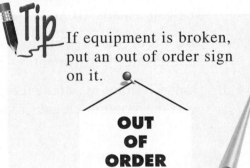

Tip If equipment is broken, put an out of order sign on it.

OUT OF ORDER

Personal Dictionary Using Machines

Write the words and phrases that you need to know.

_____

_____

_____

Listening

 **LISTEN AND WRITE**

Write the name of the machine on the maintenance report.

cash register	lawn mower	~~microwave oven~~	van

1

MAINTENANCE REPORT

Date: <u>June 1, 2000</u>

Machine: <u>microwave oven</u>

Maintenance: <u>I changed the</u>
<u>electrical cord.</u>

2

MAINTENANCE REPORT

Date: <u>July 16, 2001</u>

Machine: <u>　　　　　　</u>

Maintenance: <u>I　　　　　</u>
<u>the blades.</u>

3

MAINTENANCE REPORT

Date: <u>May 9, 1999</u>

Machine: <u>　　　　　　</u>

Maintenance: <u>I　　　　　</u>
<u>the oil.</u>

4

MAINTENANCE REPORT

Date: <u>December 3, 1999</u>

Machine: <u>　　　　　　</u>

Maintenance: <u>I　　　　a new</u>
<u>key.</u>

LISTEN AGAIN

On the maintenance report, write what each person did.

~~changed~~	changed	made	sharpened

DISCUSSION

Companies have workers complete a maintenance report after they fix something.
Why do companies ask workers to use maintenance reports?
Does your company use maintenance reports? Why?

Unit 3

Grammar ···· **Learning the language you need** ····················

A. Study the Examples

I	cleaned	the machine.
He	didn't clean	
She		
It		
We		
You		
They		

Tip Always unplug a machine before you repair it.

COMPLETE THE SENTENCES

1. We _____ *changed* _____ (**change**) the lock on the door.

2. Miguel _____ (**not wash**) the company van.

3. I _____ (**not empty**) the trash.

4. Marla _____ (**clean**) the coffee machine.

B. Study the Examples

Did	I	fix the faucet?
	you	
	he	
	she	
	we	
	they	

| Yes, | I | did. |
| No, | | didn't. |

COMPLETE THE DIALOG

A _____ *Did* _____ you _____ *fix* _____ (**fix**) the television yesterday?

B No, I _____ . I _____ (**fix**) the VCR.

A _____ you _____ (**deliver**) the VCR to the customer?

B No, I _____ . Tom _____ (**deliver**) it this morning.

PARTNER WORK

What did your partner do at work or school yesterday? Find out.
Take turns asking and answering questions. Use the language in A and B.

32

Unit 3

C. Study the Examples

I	went	to the meeting.
	didn't go	

Irregular Verbs	
bring	brought
buy	bought
go	went
have	had
make	made
send	sent
take	took

COMPLETE THE DIALOG

1. I _____went_____ (go) to the post office.

2. I _____ (buy) twenty stamps for Mrs. Li.

3. She _____ (have) several letters to send.

4. She _____ (send) them to Korea.

5. I _____ (not send) a package.

6. After the post office, I _____ (have) to go to the bank.

7. I _____ (make) a deposit for Mrs. Li

WRITE A REPORT

Finish the report about Ernesto's work.

━━━━━ WORK REPORT ━━━━━

Worker: Ernesto Peta

Date: February 12,1999

Mr. Johnson _____brought_____ (bring) a lawn mower
to the shop this morning. It _____ (have)
a broken blade. I _____ (replace) the
blade and _____ (take) the mower back
to Mr. Johnson.

PARTNER WORK

Think about a bad experience you had with a machine. What happened?
How did you fix it? Tell your partner. Share your experiences with the class.

Unit 3

READ AND WRITE

Read the service requests. Write a repair code from the list.

CITY STEAK HOUSE
REPAIR CODES

Electrical problem	**001**
Machine is old	**036**
Machine was not used correctly	**067**
Part needs replacing	**071**

---

① CITY STEAK HOUSE
SERVICE REQUEST

Name: Jun Pal

Date: March 13

Equipment: Cash register

Description: This afternoon, a customer spilled coffee on the cash register. It shorted out the machine.

For service technician only: SERVICE CODE 001

---

② CITY STEAK HOUSE
SERVICE REQUEST

Name: Wena Marcos

Date: September 19

Equipment: Kitchen door

Description: The handle on the kitchen door fell off. The door needs a new handle.

For service technician only: SERVICE CODE _____

---

③ CITY STEAK HOUSE
SERVICE REQUEST

Name: Young Kim

Date: June 4

Equipment: Mixer

Description: The low setting doesn't work. The mixer always runs on high.

For service technician only: SERVICE CODE _____

---

④ CITY STEAK HOUSE
SERVICE REQUEST

Name: Wally Sitzmann

Date: January 3

Equipment: Fire extinguisher

Description: The fire extinguisher doesn't work. The fire department says it's a 1950 model.

For service technician only: SERVICE CODE _____

Write a service request about one of these problems. Use the Useful Language. Share your request with the class.

Service Request

Name: _____

Date: _____

Equipment: _____

Description: _____

_____

_____

_____

For service technician only: SERVICE CODE _____

DISCUSSION

Work with a team. Talk about the maintenance of machines. How do you take care of these machines: cars, washing machines, ovens, televisions? Why? Share your ideas with the class.

Useful Language

It's broken.

It doesn't work.

It makes a funny noise.

Smoke is coming out of it.

It won't start.

Unit 3

READ THE USER'S MANUAL

Maintenance and Care of Your VCR 2000

1. The machine should have breathing space behind it. Keep it ten inches from the wall.

2. The cord should be against a wall.

3. Don't put liquids on or near the machine.

4. Dust the machine regularly.

5. Keep the machine out of direct sunlight.

Did they follow directions? Write *yes* or *no*.

1. Tim put the VCR in front of a sunny window. __no__

2. Alex dusted the machine every week. _____

3. Miguel put the cord along the wall. _____

4. Don pushed the machine against the wall. _____

CultureNotes

ON YOUR JOB

What do you do if you don't know how to operate a machine?
What should you do if you think a machine is not safe?

Complete the activities. Go over your work with a partner or your teacher. Then complete the Performance Review on page 38.

SKILL 1	COMPLETE A MAINTENANCE REQUEST

Your vacuum cleaner, cash register, or another machine is not working. Complete the service request. Use today's date.

Service Request

Name: _____

Date: _____

Equipment: _____

Description: _____

_____

_____

_____

_____

_____

For service technician only: **SERVICE CODE** _____

SKILL 2	TALK ABOUT PROBLEMS WITH MACHINES

Think of a problem with a machine at your workplace or school. Who can you ask for help? What do you say? Tell your partner or your teacher.

Are they following the user's manual? Write *yes* or *no*.

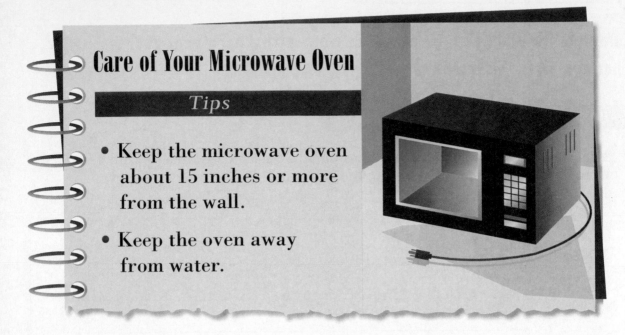

Care of Your Microwave Oven

Tips

- Keep the microwave oven about 15 inches or more from the wall.

- Keep the oven away from water.

1. Lin put the microwave oven 15 inches from the wall. _____

2. Al put a glass of water on top of the microwave. _____

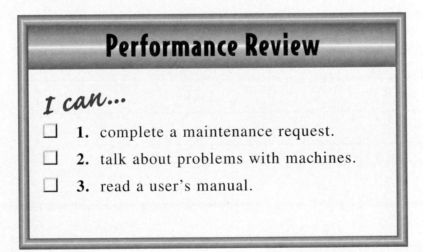

Performance Review

I can...

☐ **1.** complete a maintenance request.

☐ **2.** talk about problems with machines.

☐ **3.** read a user's manual.

Discussion

Work with a team. How will your new skills help you? Make a list. Share your list with the class.

What do you think?

Look at the schedules.

Do you use schedules at work?

How do you manage your time?

Performance Preview

Can you...

☐ 1. understand schedules?

☐ 2. interpret a holiday schedule?

☐ 3. use calendars and planners?

TEAM WORK

Look at the schedule and the to-do list. Decide when to do the tasks on the to-do list. Add them to the schedule.

Wednesday, December 2		Thursday, December 3	
7:00	7 to 1 Work first shift		7:00
8:00			8:00
9:00			9:00
10:00			10:00
11:00		11 to 3 Work second shift	11:00
12:00			12:00
1:00			1:00
2:00			2:00
3:00			3:00
4:00		4 to 6 English class	4:00
5:00	Doctor's appointment,		5:00
6:00	5 to 7		6:00
7:00			7:00

 PRACTICE THE DIALOG

A How about 6:00 on Thursday?

B Sorry, I'm busy then. How about 2:00 on Wednesday?

A That sounds great!

Now work with a partner from a different team. Look at your team's schedule. Use the dialog to set up a meeting to discuss a class project.

TO DO

Immigration Office—2 hours

Buy birthday presents for
   kids—1 hour

Send special order—1 hour

Mail catalogs to
   customers—2 hours

 **SURVEY**

How many students prefer first shift? How many students prefer second shift? Ask six classmates. Share the information with the class.

Talk About It

Finest Furniture Corporation
Daily Schedule

Name: **Pedro**

Tuesday, April 4

8:45 to 9:15	Daily schedule review
9:15 to 9:45	Loading
9:45 to 10:15	Vehicle check
10:15 to 12:30	Deliveries, north/west
12:30 to 1:15	Lunch
1:15 to 3:00	Deliveries, south/east
3:30 to 4:30	Department safety meeting

Schedule Changes

1. Add north side delivery after 1:00

2. 5pm–Shipment arrives– Get unloading help

3. Pick up package at airport – 12:30.

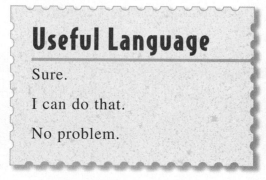

PRACTICE THE DIALOG

A Pedro, can you add a delivery to the north side after 1:00?

B I don't think so. I have to make deliveries on the south side then.

Useful Language

Sure.

I can do that.

No problem.

PARTNER WORK

Look at the schedule and the schedule changes on the clipboard. Talk about adding the changes to the schedule. Use the dialog and Useful Language above.

ASAP PROJECT

Plan a schedule for studying English. Form study teams with 3 students in each team. Choose times and places to study together. Write your study schedule. Share it with the class. Complete this project as you work through this unit.

Bell Fashions Annual Sale
8:00 to 10:00

1. Put sale signs in the windows.
2. Put clothes on the shelves and racks.
3. Put sale signs in the store.

10:00 Open the store.

PRACTICE THE DIALOG

A What are we going to do first on Monday morning?

B First, we're going to put sale signs in the windows.

Continue to talk about the schedule. Use the dialog and the Useful Language.

Useful Language

first   second   then

Tip When you get a new schedule, read it completely. Then ask questions to make sure you understand.

Personal Dictionary > Following Schedules

Write the words and phrases that you need to know.

_____

_____

Listening

Understanding schedules and deadlines

 LISTEN AND MATCH

What needs to be done in each meeting room? Write the letter next to the room.

1. Lake Room _____d_____   **a.** 50 round tables and 600 chairs

2. Meeting Room 1 _____   **b.** 2 long tables, 20 chairs, and a VCR

3. Meeting Room 2 _____   **c.** 1 table and 10 chairs

4. Grand Ballroom _____   **d.** 300 chairs

LISTEN AGAIN

Write the deadline for each task.

1. Lake Room _____9:00_____

2. Meeting Room 1 _____

3. Meeting Room 2 _____

4. Grand Ballroom _____

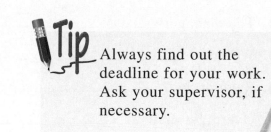

Tip Always find out the deadline for your work. Ask your supervisor, if necessary.

LISTEN AND WRITE

When are the customers' appointments? Write the names on the schedule.

~~Ellen North~~   Donna   Hong   Mrs. Matesa

Lewis's Beauty Shop

9:00 _____

10:00 _Ellen North_____

11:00 _____

12:00 _____

Learning the language you need

A. Study the Examples

I We You They	have to don't have to	deliver these packages.
He She	has to doesn't have to	deliver these packages.

COMPLETE THE SENTENCES

1. Workers _____have to open_____ (**open**) mail every day.

2. The manager _____ (**not explain**) special tasks.

3. Workers _____ (**put**) postage on all mail.

4. Regular mail _____ (**not be**) ready until 3:30.

5. Overnight mail _____ (**be**) ready by 1:30.

6. Customers _____ (**not send**) packages first class.

7. _____ we _____ (**go**) to the post office every day?

8. Yes, you _____ (**take**) the packages there every day at 3:30.

B. Study the Examples

Do	I we you they	have to sign the attendance sheet?
Does	he she	

TEAM WORK

What do you have to do? Ask and answer questions about your workplaces.

1. punch in on a time clock

2. work on weekends

3. go to department meetings

4. get to work early

Unit 4

C. Study the examples

I'm	going to be late.
We're	
You're	
They're	

He's	going to be late.
She's	
It's	

When	are you going to do it?
Why	

COMPLETE THE DIALOG

Read the fire station schedule.

Sandy Point Fire Department

Station Projects, March 3-8

Monday	Put a new hose on truck 48
Tuesday	Department meeting
Wednesday	Test hard hats
Thursday	Clean truck 66
Friday	Change smoke detector batteries

A When ____are____ we ____going to test____ (**test**) the hard hats?

B We _____ (**test**) them on Wednesday.

A What _____ we _____ (**do**) on Monday?

B We _____ (**put**) a new hose on truck 48.

TEAM WORK

Work in two teams. Read Pablo's schedule. Write questions about it.
Give your questions to the other team. Answer the other team's questions.

Pablo	*Reliable Delivery Service*

Wednesday, April 5
8:45 to 9:15   review schedule
9:15 to 9:45   load truck
9:45 to 10:15   check the truck
10:15 to 1:15   make deliveries
1:15 to 2:00   eat lunch
2:00 to 4:30   make deliveries

Reading and Writing

READ CARMEN'S TO-DO LIST

TO DO

1. Buy colored paper.

2. Check lamp prices.

3. Buy envelopes.

4. Put chairs in warehouse.

5. Get two new desk calendars.

6. Organize supply room

7. Put together new paper cutters.

8. Buy bookshelf for Mr. Smith's office.

9. Put extra boxes in warehouse.

10. Return damaged chair to furniture store.

ORGANIZE THE TASKS

Today Carmen is going to go to the company warehouse, an office supply store, and a furniture store. Organize her list to help her save time. Put the number of the item under the place. There are 2 things she has to do at other places. Circle them.

warehouse	office supply store	furniture store
	1,	

DISCUSSION

What do you do to save time? Share your ideas with the class.

What do you have to do next week? Write your schedule for next week

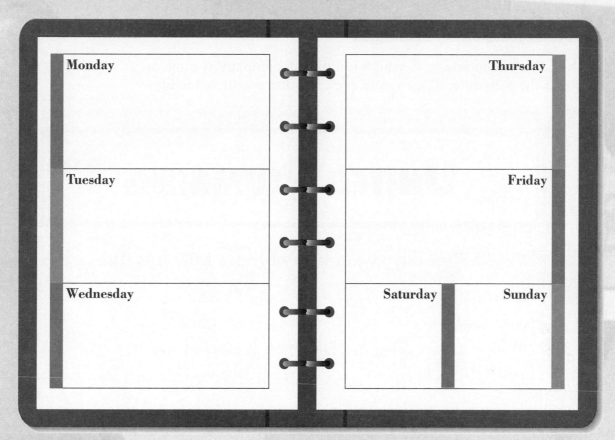

PARTNER WORK

Share your calendar with your partner.
Talk about what you have to do
next week. Who is busier?

Tip After you make an
appointment or find
out a deadline,
write it down.

Discussion

Are calendars and planners helpful? Why? Do you use one now?
Why or why not? How do you think a planner can help you?
Give examples.

READ THE HOLIDAY SCHEDULE

A holiday schedule tells which holidays a company is closed.
Read the schedule. Then circle each holiday on the calendars.

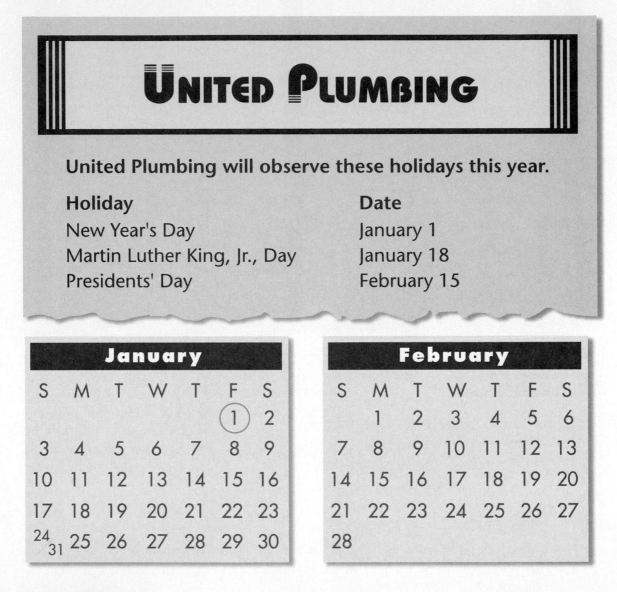

UNITED PLUMBING

United Plumbing will observe these holidays this year.

Holiday	Date
New Year's Day	January 1
Martin Luther King, Jr., Day	January 18
Presidents' Day	February 15

January

S	M	T	W	T	F	S
					①	2
3	4	5	6	7	8	9
10	11	12	13	14	15	16
17	18	19	20	21	22	23
24 31	25	26	27	28	29	30

February

S	M	T	W	T	F	S
	1	2	3	4	5	6
7	8	9	10	11	12	13
14	15	16	17	18	19	20
21	22	23	24	25	26	27
28						

 Culture Notes

What holidays do you have in your country? Are banks and schools in your country closed on those holidays? When are banks and schools closed in this country? Does your workplace close those same days?

How well can you use the skills in this unit?

Complete the activities. Go over your work with a partner or your teacher. Then complete the Performance Review on page 50.

SKILL 1 **UNDERSTAND SCHEDULES**

Answer the questions about Ruben's schedule.

Tuesday, March 13

7:00	1:00 **1:00 - 2:00 choose new materials**
8:00 **8:00 - 9:00 department meeting**	2:00
9:00 **9:00 - 10:00 meet new employees**	3:00 **3:00 - 5:00 finish Santos project :**
10:00 **10:00 - 12:00 attend client**	4:00 **due tomorrow morning!**
11:00 **presentation**	5:00
12:00 **12:00 - 1:00 lunch with Felipe**	6:00

1. What time is Ruben going to meet new employees? _____

2. Does Ruben have time for another meeting in the morning? _____

3. What time is Ruben free in the afternoon? _____

SKILL 2 **INTERPRET A HOLIDAY SCHEDULE**

November 28–29 . . . . . Thanksgiving
December 25 . . . . Christmas

1. It's November 27. Is the company open? _____

2. It's December 24. Is the company open? _____

3. It's December 25. Is the company open? _____

Unit 4

Write your schedule for one week.

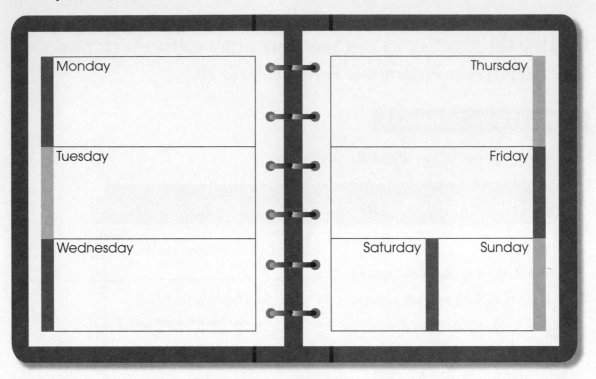

Monday	Thursday
Tuesday	Friday
Wednesday	Saturday / Sunday

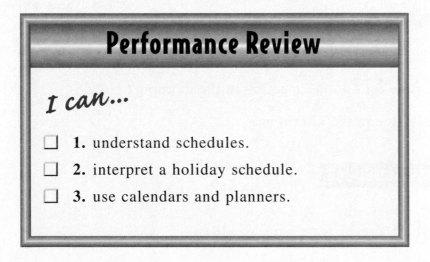

Performance Review

I can...

☐ **1.** understand schedules.

☐ **2.** interpret a holiday schedule.

☐ **3.** use calendars and planners.

DISCUSSION

Work with a team. How will your new skills help you? Make a list.
Share your list with the class.

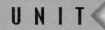

What do you think?

Look at the pictures.

What's happening in each picture?

What requests are the people making?

Performance Preview

Can you...

☐ 1. respond to requests?

☐ 2. handle special requests?

☐ 3. offer suggestions?

☐ 4. understand customer service policies?

TEAM WORK

Choose an answer for each picture. Discuss your choices with the class.

> a. Yes, I'd be happy to.
>
> ✗ b. I'm not sure. I need to check my schedule.
>
> c. I'm sorry. We give store credit only.

Can you deliver the boxes today?

Can you give me some towels?

Can I get a cash refund?

PARTNER WORK

Student A is a hotel guest. Student B is an employee.
Student A makes requests. Student B responds.

A Can you get me two more pillows?

B Of course. I'll be right back.

SURVEY

What are some common requests you get at work? Talk to your classmates about them. List three of the most common requests.

Talk About It

PRACTICE THE DIALOG

A I finished putting down the carpet.

B When did you finish?

A Just before lunch. I need to clean up now.

B What can we do with this extra carpet?

A We can put it in the closet in the reception area.

B That's a good idea.

Useful Language

Why don't I...?

What about...?

Why not...?

Let's....

PARTNER WORK

You're the carpet layer. Your partner is the office manager. Talk about what else to do with the extra carpet. Use the dialog and Useful Language above.

ASAP
PROJECT

As a class, think of requests at your workplace or school. Divide into teams. One team thinks of requests. The other team makes suggestions for responding to the requests. Make a chart of the requests and responses. Complete this project as you work through this unit.

PRACTICE THE DIALOG

A Can I have extra cheese on my hamburger?

B Sure, anything else?

A Can I have salad instead of French fries?

B Sorry, we don't have salad.

Student A makes more requests.
Student B responds. Use the dialog
and the Useful Language

Useful Language

Of course.

No problem.

Sorry, I can't make
substitutions.

Personal Dictionary ▶ Serving Customers

Write the words and phrases that you need to know.

_____

_____

_____

Listening

Dealing with special requests

LISTEN AND CIRCLE

Where are the speakers?

1.	(a restaurant)	a factory
2.	a clothes store	a new car lot
3.	a copy shop	a bus
4.	a furniture store	a barber shop
5.	a hospital	an electronics store

LISTEN AGAIN

Match the request and the response.

Requests

___e___ 1. Replace the coleslaw with a salad.

_____ 2. Get a refund.

_____ 3. Stop at the Speedy Mail store.

_____ 4. Get the tables by Saturday morning.

_____ 5. Bring up the stereo from storage.

Responses

a. The manager will decide.

b. The driver will stop when the bus gets there.

c. They'll be the first delivery on Saturday.

d. He already brought it up.

e. There are no substitutions.

DISCUSSION

Look at the requests and responses in Listen Again. Did the employees provide good customer service? Why do you think so? If necessary, listen to the conversations again.

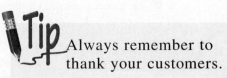

Tip Always remember to thank your customers.

A. Study the Examples

Where	did you	buy this machine?
When		call the service center?
How		fix it?

I	bought it at the downtown store.
	called last week.
	fixed it with a new part.

Irregular Verbs	
buy	bought
do	did
find	found
get	got
make	made
pay	paid
see	saw
wear	wore
tell	told

COMPLETE THE CONVERSATION

Write *where*, *when*, or *how*. Write the correct form of the verb.

1. **A** _____Where_____ did you find that jacket?

   B I _____found_____ (**find**) it at a discount store downtown.

2. **A** _____ did you buy it?

   B I _____ (**buy**) it on Thursday.

3. **A** _____ did you pay for it?

   B I _____ (**pay**) for it with a check.

4. **A** _____ did you wear it?

   B I _____ (**wear**) it to the job interview.

5. **A** _____ did you get the job?

   B I _____ (**get**) the job on Friday.

 PARTNER WORK

Work with a partner. Talk about something that you bought for work or school. When did you buy it? Where? How did you buy it?

B. Study the Examples

Did	you	help the customer?		Yes,	I	did.
	he			No,		didn't.

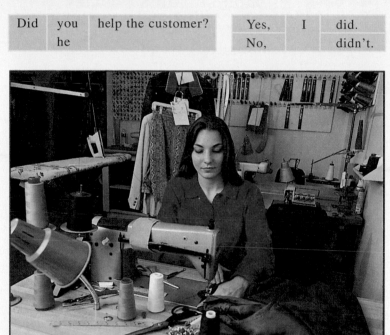

COMPLETE THE DIALOG

Write *did* or *didn't*.

A _____Did_____ Maria pin the cloth?

B Yes, she _____did_____ .

A _____ she cut it?

B Yes, she _____ .

A _____ she sew it?

B Yes, she _____ .

A _____ she put on the buttons?

B No, she _____ .

A _____ she iron the coat?

B No, she _____ .

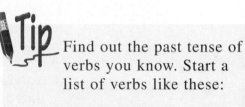

Tip Find out the past tense of verbs you know. Start a list of verbs like these:

do	did
cut	cut
have	had

PARTNER WORK

Student A asks a question about work. Student B answers the question.

A Did you sell a radio today?

B Yes, I did.

Reading and Writing

READ THE RETURN POLICY

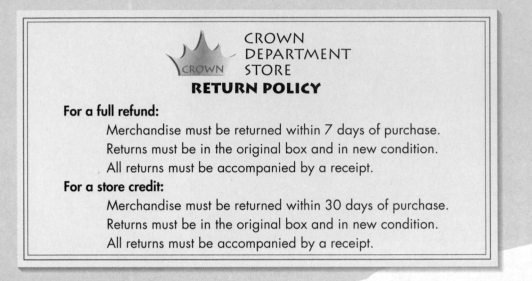

CROWN DEPARTMENT STORE

RETURN POLICY

For a full refund:

Merchandise must be returned within 7 days of purchase.

Returns must be in the original box and in new condition.

All returns must be accompanied by a receipt.

For a store credit:

Merchandise must be returned within 30 days of purchase.

Returns must be in the original box and in new condition.

All returns must be accompanied by a receipt.

WRITE THE ANSWER

Look at the store Return Policy. Read about the customers' returns.
Write *refund*, *store credit*, or *no return*.

_____refund_____ **1.** Jill Volpe returned a coat three days after she bought it.
It was the wrong color. It was new and in the original box.
She had the receipt.

_____ **2.** Yolanda Bueno returned a stereo seven days after she bought it.
She didn't have the receipt.

_____ **3.** Rosa Mendoza returned a pair of shoes two weeks after she
bought them. They were the wrong size. She had the receipt.
The shoes were still in the box. They were new.

_____ **4.** Minnie Li returned a toy car one week after she bought it.
The toy car didn't work. She had the receipt. It was in the box.
It was new.

DISCUSSION

How long should customers keep receipts? Why?
Is returning something easy? Why? Are stores' policies usually clear?

Unit 5

Use the receipts and the information on page 58 to complete the refund forms for Rosa Mendoza and Minnie Li. Follow the example. The date is June 15.

CROWN DEPARTMENT STORE

RETURN FORM

Date of sale _June 12_   Date of Return _June 15_

Merchandise _Coat_

Reason _The coat was the wrong color._

Total Amount Due _$79.99_

Customer Signature _Jill Volpe_

Refund _✓_   Store Credit _____

Crown Department Store
Woodbridge Mall

June 12

Coat $79.99
Total   **$79.99**

CROWN DEPARTMENT STORE

RETURN FORM

Date of sale _____   Date of Return _____

Merchandise _____

Reason _____

Total Amount Due _____

Customer Signature _____

Refund _____   Store Credit _____

Crown Department Store
Woodbridge Mall

June 1

Shoes $75.75
Total   **$75.75**

CROWN DEPARTMENT STORE

RETURN FORM

Date of sale _____   Date of Return _____

Merchandise _____

Reason _____

Total Amount Due _____

Customer Signature _____

Refund _____   Store Credit _____

Crown Department Store
Woodbridge Mall

June 8

Toy car $19.95
Total   **$19.95**

Unit 5

READ AND CIRCLE

Read each customer's request. Choose the better response.
Talk about it with your classmates.

1. Can I get a box of paper clips?

   a. They come in boxes of 1,000 and 5,000. Which size box do you want?

   b. Which size box?

2. Can I leave my car in the no-parking zone for just a minute?

   a. It's really not a good idea. This is an emergency exit.

   b. No. Move your car now.

3. Would you please make twenty copies of this report? I need them right away.

   a. Can't you see I'm busy?

   b. Dana says she doesn't need her copies right away. I'll make yours now.

4. This toaster broke the first time I used it. May I talk to the manager?

   a. Why do you think it's our responsibility?

   b. I'm sure the manager can help you. Do you have your receipt?

5. John, please take this food to table ten.

   a. Sure. Just let me put this coffee pot down.

   b. I'm a cook, not a waiter.

TEAM WORK

Think of more good ways to answer these requests.
Share them with the class.

 *Culture Notes*

Why is good customer service important? What happens to companies
that offer poor service?

Performance Check
How well can you use the skills
in this unit?

Complete the activities. Go over your work with a partner or your teacher.
Then complete the Performance Review on page 62.

SKILL 1 | **RESPOND TO REQUESTS**

Your partner or teacher wants you to help move the furniture in your classroom.
How do you respond?

SKILL 2 | **HANDLE SPECIAL REQUESTS**

Read The Copy Shop's store policies and the customer's special requests.
What do you say? Talk about it with your teacher or partner.

1. A customer wants ten copies right away.

2. A customer wants 1,000 copies. He doesn't have money to pay in advance.

STORE POLICIES

1. Allow at least one hour for all copy orders.

2. Orders of 500 copies or more must be paid for in advance.

SKILL 3 | **OFFER SUGGESTIONS**

You work at Quality Supermarket. A customer does not know what to fix for
dinner. Make one or two suggestions. Follow the example:

How about hamburgers?

Crystal Dining Elegance Return Policy

- A full refund is available on returns within 30 days of purchase.

- All returns must be accompanied by a receipt.

- In-store credits are available on returns within 45 days of purchase.

- After 45 days, no credits and no returns are available.

Read the policy. Write *refund*, *store credit*, or *no return*.

_____ **1.** Kathy wants to return some water glasses she bought last week. She did not use them. She has the receipt.

_____ **2.** Ralph wants to return some plates he bought six months ago. He has the receipt.

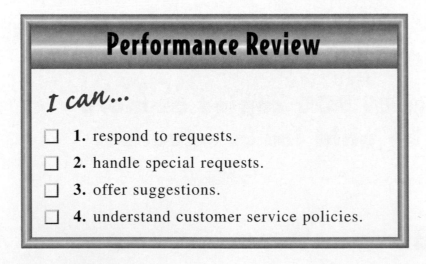

Performance Review

I can...

- ☐ **1.** respond to requests.
- ☐ **2.** handle special requests.
- ☐ **3.** offer suggestions.
- ☐ **4.** understand customer service policies.

DISCUSSION

Work with a team. How will your new skills help you? Make a list.
Share your list with the class.

OUR MISSION is to:
- Provide quality hair care
- Create satisfied customers
- Offer competitive prices
- Earn customer's respect

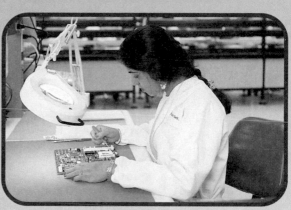

What do you think?

Look at the pictures.

What do you see?

Do you see scenes like these at your workplace?

Performance Preview

Can you...

- ☐ 1. follow rules?
- ☐ 2. make compromises?
- ☐ 3. understand company goals?
- ☐ 4. get along with others?

TEAM WORK

Read the memos. Choose a subject for each one. Share your answers.

Checking out supplies	**Being on time**
Parking	~~Smoking~~

MEMO

To: All Employees   **Date:** 8-19

From: Francisco Vega, Building Manager

Re: _Smoking_

Effective September 1, smoking will not be allowed anywhere on company property, including the parking lots and the picnic area.

MEMO

To: All Packagers   **Date:** 4-3

From: Katya Taylor, Manager

Re: _____

Only two workers arrived late in March. That's good! Let's all try to be on time every day in April.

MEMO

To: All Employees   **Date:** 12-12

From: Valentino Santos, Security Manager

Re: _____

Visitor parking spaces are for customers only. Employees may not use the visitor parking spaces at any time.

MEMO

To: All Support Staff   **Date:** 2-9

From: Latifa Tahiri, Office Manager

Re: _____

Please fill out the check out list when taking supplies from the supply room.

PARTNER WORK

Talk about the memos. Student A asks about a rule. Student B says it.

A What's the rule about parking?

B Visitor parking spaces are for customers only.

 **SURVEY**

Make a list of rules at your workplace or school.
Think of the reasons for the rules. Make a second list.

Talk About It

Compromising

PRACTICE THE DIALOG

A Lee, we're going to be busier than usual tomorrow. Can you work from 7:00 to 12:00?

B I'm sorry, Virginia, I can't. My daughter has a doctor's appointment at 11:00.

A That's too bad. We have a lot of big holiday orders.

B I could come in from 6:00 to 9:00.

A That would help a lot. Thanks, Lee.

B No problem, Virginia.

Useful Language

I can't do it this time.

I can come in for a couple of hours.

How about. . . ?

Sure.

That sounds good.

PARTNER WORK

Ask your partner to work on Wednesday. Use the dialog and Useful Language above.

ASAP PROJECT

As a class, write rules and goals for your class. Make rules, such as "Be on time." Make goals, such as "Learn ten new words a week." Everybody should agree on all items. Post the list on your classroom wall. Complete this project as you work through this unit.

Keep Talking

PARTNER WORK

Look at the pictures. What's the matter?

 PRACTICE THE DIALOG

A Excuse me, your smoke is coming in the window. Could you please smoke somewhere else?

B Sorry, I'll go over there.

Now talk about the other pictures above. Student A makes requests. Student B responds. Use the dialog and the Useful Language.

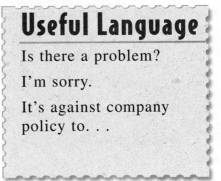

Useful Language

Is there a problem?

I'm sorry.

It's against company policy to. . .

Personal Dictionary ▶ Fitting in at Work

Write the words and phrases that you need to know.

_____

_____

_____

Listening
Doing good work
···

 LISTEN AND CIRCLE

Listen and circle what the boss says during the performance review in column A.

	A	**B**
Mary	good attitude	raise
	always on time	no promotion
	very responsible	promotion
Lester	very reliable	raise
	careful worker	no promotion
	often late	promotion

 LISTEN AGAIN

What happens? Circle the answer in column B.

 **LISTEN AND CIRCLE**

Circle all the reasons Sergio is Employee of the Year.

never absent	very polite
comes in early	helps others
does good work	honest
friendly	cooperative
hard-working	thinks about details

Discussion

What is excellent work behavior? Is Sergio's work behavior excellent? Why? Do you know someone who has excellent work habits? Who? What are that person's habits?

Grammar Learning the language you need

A. Study the Examples

The new trucks are	faster bigger heavier nicer better worse	than the old ones.

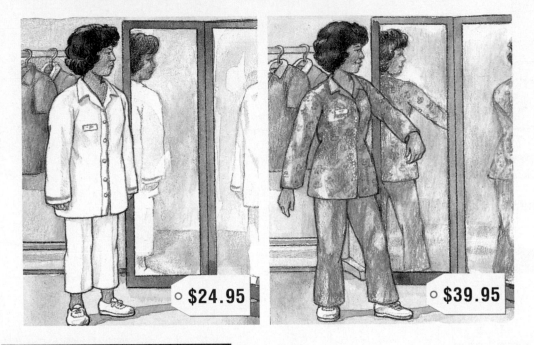

$24.95

$39.95

COMPLETE THE SENTENCES

Ana needs a new uniform for work. Complete the sentences.

1. The pink pants are ___*longer than*___ (**long**) the white pants.

2. The white pants are _____ (**short**) the pink pants.

3. The white blouse is _____ (**large**) the pink blouse.

4. The pink blouse is _____ (**small**) the white blouse.

5. The white uniform is _____ (**cheap**) the pink uniform.

6. The pink uniform is _____ (**pretty**) the white uniform.

7. The pink uniform is _____ (**better**) the white uniform.

B. Study the Examples

| This shirt is | more expensive than
more comfortable than | that shirt. |

Tip Use "-er" to make comparisons with short words:

fast, faster   tall, taller

Use "more" to make comparisons with longer words:

beautiful, more beautiful
difficult, more difficult

○ $30.00

○ $9.99

PARTNER WORK

Talk about the two shirts. Use these words:

practical   expensive   formal   colorful   comfortable

A This shirt is more colorful than that one.

B Yes, it is. But that shirt is more comfortable.

COMPLETE THE SENTENCES

Use the language in A and B.

1. Joe's work is ___*more careful than*___ (**careful**) Al's work.

2. The electric drill is _____ (**noise**) the hand drill.

3. Ali's _____ (**friendly**) John.

4. This company is _____ (**large**) that store.

5. I want a job in the sales department. It's _____ (**interesting**) the production department.

6. Goggles are _____ (**safe**) regular glasses.

7. A forklift is _____ (**dangerous**) than a hand truck.

Unit 6

Reading and Writing

READ THE COMPANY HANDBOOK

Northwest Distribution Company

Company Rules

1. Except in case of emergency, employees may not make or receive personal phone calls.
2. No personal visitors are allowed during office hours.
3. Office hours are 8 am to 5 pm.
4. Each employee may take one 30-minute lunch break between 11:30 and 1:00.
5. Each employee may take a 15-minute break between 9:30 and 10:30 and between 2:30 and 3:30.
6. Employees are expected to be on time arriving for work and returning from breaks. Being late more than 3 times is grounds for dismissal.

PARTNER WORK

Which rule did they break? Write the number.

1. Rick called his daughter in Florida. Yesterday was her birthday. ___1___

2. Marion always goes out to lunch with her boyfriend. Sometimes he waits for her in the reception area. _____

3. Ellen calls her husband every hour. _____

4. Ed was 15 minutes late three days this week. _____

5. Lisa took her break at 9:15. _____

6. Susan ate lunch at 1:15. _____

7. Todd left work at 4:30. _____

DISCUSSION

Work with a team. Talk about policies at your workplace or school. Why are the policies important?

Work with a team. Imagine your workplace or school is having some problems. Workers are late from breaks, make personal photocopies, smoke in the rest rooms, and park in the visitors' parking lot. Write rules to correct the problems.

1.	Workers may not return late from breaks.

 TEAM WORK

Think of some rules for your workplace or school.
Make a list.

Extension

Understanding company goals

READ THE MISSION STATEMENT

A company's mission statement tells employees the company's goals.

Express Delivery Company

Our Mission Is To

- Deliver each and every package on time
- Keep packages safe and clean
- Offer competitive rates
- Greet customers with a smile
- Answer customers' questions politely
- Handle customers' special requests

WRITE *YES* OR *NO*

Are the employees following Express Delivery Company's mission?

___no___ **1.** It's five o'clock. A driver doesn't deliver the last three packages on the schedule.

_____ **2.** A customer asks for a weekend delivery. A clerk says he will find a driver to make the delivery.

_____ **3.** A clerk smiles and says, "May I help you?"

_____ **4.** A driver delivers a package on a specific day by customer request.

_____ **5.** A driver leaves packages in the rain.

ON YOUR JOB Culture Notes

When you see a worker who isn't following company rules, what do you do? Why?

Complete the activities. Go over your work with a partner or your teacher.
Then complete the Performance Review on page 74.

SKILL 1   FOLLOW RULES

Work starts at 9:00, and employees must fill out the check-out list when they get supplies. Tell your teacher which employees are following the rules.

SKILL 2   MAKE COMPROMISES

Your partner or teacher asks you to work an extra day next week.
You have plans for that afternoon. What do you say?

Unit 6

73

UNDERSTAND COMPANY GOALS

Circle Fabric House's goals.

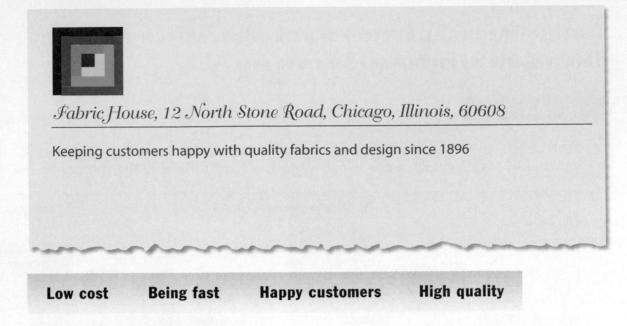

Fabric House, 12 North Stone Road, Chicago, Illinois, 60608

Keeping customers happy with quality fabrics and design since 1896

Low cost   **Being fast**   **Happy customers**   **High quality**

SKILL 4   **GET ALONG WITH OTHERS**

You are listening to music. Your teacher or partner says that the music is too loud. What do you say?

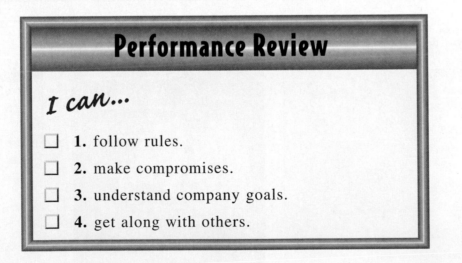

Performance Review

I can...

☐ **1.** follow rules.

☐ **2.** make compromises.

☐ **3.** understand company goals.

☐ **4.** get along with others.

Discussion

Work with a team. How will your new skills help you? Make a list. Share your list with the class.

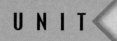
Finances

What do you think?

Look at the pictures.

What are the people doing?

When are you paid?

Where can you get these forms?

Performance Preview

Can you...

- [ ] 1. understand a paycheck?
- [ ] 2. report mistakes in your paycheck?
- [ ] 3. understand information about Social Security?
- [ ] 4. understand a W-2 form?

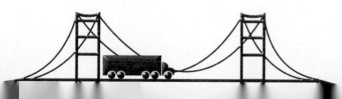

TEAM WORK

Look at the paycheck stub. Put the words into the correct list.

earnings	federal tax	gross pay	health insurance
life insurance	net pay	state tax	

✚ MERCY HOSPITAL

RATE	HOURS	EARNINGS	YEAR TO DATE
$9.40	80.00	$752.00	$12,784.00

GROSS PAY $752.00
PAY PERIOD BEGINNING   09/01/99
PAY PERIOD ENDING   09/15/99

DEDUCTIONS	
Federal tax	$90.24
State tax	60.16
FICA	36.00
Medicare	6.00
Health insurance	14.20
Life insurance	2.60
TOTAL DEDUCTIONS	$209.20
NET PAY	$542.80

Pay	**Benefits**	**Taxes**
earnings	_____	_____
_____	_____	_____
_____		

PARTNER WORK

Student A asks questions about the paycheck. Student B answers.

A How much is the gross pay?

B It's $752.

SURVEY

Talk to 5 classmates. How many have had a mistake on a paycheck?
Was the mistake large? What did the company do about the mistake?
Report your findings to the class.

Talk About It

Talking about pay

PRACTICE THE DIALOG

A At Service Plastics, payday is every Friday, and your pay rate is $6.50 an hour.

B Excuse me. Could you repeat that?

A Of course. Payday is every Friday. Your pay rate is $6.50 an hour.

B Can I start soon?

A Sure, you can start today. Your shift starts at 5:00, so be here at least 10 minutes before 5:00.

Tip When you get a new job, find out your pay rate, the start date, and time your shift starts.

PARTNER WORK

You're the boss. Tell your partner that payday is every Thursday. The rate of pay is $7 an hour and the shift starts at 3:00. Use the dialog above. Then switch roles. Talk about other pay rates and start times.

ASAP PROJECT

As a team, gather important tax and payroll forms. Use them to create a class reference booklet. Include information on where to get the forms, how to fill them out, and when to file them.

 PRACTICE THE DIALOG

A Mr. Reynosa, I think there's a mistake in my paycheck.

B Can I see it?

A Here it is. Last week I worked 30 hours, but my paycheck is for only 24 hours.

B You're right. Let me check your timecard.

A OK.

B Hmm. It's because you worked 6 hours on Saturday. Those hours go on your next paycheck.

A Oh, I see. Thanks.

> **Tip** If you think there's a mistake with your paycheck, talk to your boss or Human Resources right away.

 PARTNER WORK

You worked 40 hours last week, but your paycheck is for 30 hours. Tell your partner. Follow the dialog above.

Personal Dictionary ▶ Understanding Finances

Write the words and phrases that you need to know.

_____

_____

_____

Unit 7

Listening

Understanding a paycheck

LISTEN AND CIRCLE

What are the people asking about? Circle the letter.

1. **a.** life insurance   (**b.**) overtime pay

2. **a.** pay rate   **b.** number of hours

3. **a.** health insurance   **b.** pay rate

4. **a.** federal tax   **b.** state tax

5. **a.** overtime pay   **b.** paycheck

LISTEN AGAIN

Complete the explanation. Write the letter.

1. Overtime pay is separate from regular pay because ___a___ .

    a. the pay rate is different.

    b. the tax rate is different.

2. Jack's paycheck is high because _____ .

    a. he was not late.

    b. he worked more hours.

3. Vivian will _____ .

    a. call Bita later today.

    b. find out about the health insurance deduction.

4. Don needs to _____ .

    a. check with Human Resources.

    b. check with the employee's boss.

5. Christine has to go to Human Resources to _____ .

    a. fill out a form.

    b. pick up her paycheck.

Grammar · Learning the language you need

A. Study the Examples

Could you	look at my paycheck? answer a question?

COMPLETE THE QUESTIONS

Use the language in A.

1. ___Could you check___ (**check**) my W-4 form?

2. _____ (**change**) the amount of my deduction?

3. _____ (**show**) me my gross pay?

4. _____ (**tell**) me my net pay?

COMPLETE THE DIALOG

Use the language in A.

show	repeat	~~answer~~

> **Tip** Save your pay stubs from your paychecks. Keep them all together. Use them to check your paychecks.

A ___Could you answer___ a question about my paycheck?

B Sure. Go ahead.

A Well, I get paid $7.00 an hour, and I worked 25 hours last week.

B _____ that? How many hours?

A 25. So my gross pay should be $175. But it's $200.

B OK. _____ me your paycheck?

A Yes. Here it is.

B Let's see. Your pay went up because you sold a $250 camera. You got a $25 bonus.

A Oh, great! Thanks.

B. Study the Examples

> I need to talk to my supervisor because I want to go on vacation.
> I want to go on vacation, so I need to talk to my supervisor.

COMPLETE THE SENTENCES

Use *because* or *so*.

1. Eduardo always reads his paycheck _____because_____ he wants to understand it.

2. Carmen, his wife, reads it too _____ she wants to make sure it's correct.

3. Once they found a mistake in Eduardo's paycheck,

   _____ Eduardo called Human Resources.

4. The employees in Human Resources thanked Eduardo for

   calling _____ there was a mistake on the check.

5. His paycheck was low, _____ Human Resources gave him a new check.

COMPLETE THE SENTENCES

Use *because* or *so*.

Tim had some questions about his paycheck, _____so_____

he talked to his boss. She told him his pay went up _____

he was on time every day. But his taxes went up _____

he made more money. Also, he has new health insurance, _____

his pay went down a little. Tim is happy he talked to his boss

_____ now he understands his paycheck.

 PARTNER WORK

Take turns talking to your boss about the situations.
Use *because* and *so* to explain your reasons.

1. You want to go on vacation next month.

2. You need to arrive late tomorrow.

Unit 7

READ

Social Security Helps Millions of People

Social Security is a large goverment program that helps people who are not able to work. Social Security also helps some families after the husband or wife dies. Social Security pays cash benefits, usually in the form of a monthly check. Social Security is paid out of deductions from workers' paychecks. If you work in the United States, you have to pay Social Security taxes. Social Security helps millions of people. Right now over 49 million people get Social Security benefits.

WRITE YES OR NO

1. Social Security is a government program. _yes_

2. Social Security helps only people who are older. _____

3. Taxes help pay for Social Security. _____

4. Very few people get Social Security benefits. _____

5. All workers in the United States pay Social Security taxes. _____

DISCUSSION

How do you feel about the taxes you pay? Do you think you pay too much in taxes? What services do your taxes pay for? Do you use any of these services?

To work in the U.S., you need a Social Security card. To get a card, you have to fill out a form. Here is part of the form. Fill it out.

SOCIAL SECURITY ADMINISTRATION
Application for a Social Security Card

INSTRUCTIONS
- Please read "How To Complete This Form" on page 2.
- Print or type using black or blue ink. DO NOT USE PENCIL.
- After you complete this form, take or mail it along with the required documents to your nearest Social Security office.
- If you are completing this form for someone else, answer the questions as they apply to that person. Then, sign your name in question 16.

1 NAME
To Be Shown On Card

FIRST | FULL MIDDLE NAME | LAST

2 MAILING ADDRESS

STREET ADDRESS, APT. NO., PO BOX, RURAL ROUTE NO.

CITY | STATE | ZIP CODE

3 CITIZENSHIP (Check One)

☐ U.S. Citizen | ☐ Legal Alien Allowed To Work | ☐ Legal Alien Not Allowed To Work | ☐ Foreign Student | ☐ Conditionally Legalized Alien | ☐ Other

4 SEX

☐ Male | ☐ Female

5 RACE/ETHNIC DESCRIPTION (Check One Only–Voluntary)

☐ Asian, Asian-American Or Pacific Islander | ☐ Hispanic | ☐ Black (Not Hispanic) | ☐ North American Indian Or Alaskan Native | ☐ White (Not Hispanic)

6 DATE OF BIRTH _____ MONTH DAY YEAR

7 PLACE OF BIRTH _____ CITY _____ STATE OR FOREIGN COUNTRY _____ FCI

Office Use Only

8 MOTHER'S MAIDEN NAME

FIRST | FULL MIDDLE NAME | LAST NAME AT HER BIRTH

9 FATHER'S NAME

FIRST | FULL MIDDLE NAME | LAST

16 YOUR SIGNATURE

17 YOUR RELATIONSHIP TO THE PERSON IN ITEM 1 IS:

☐ Self | ☐ Natural or Adoptive Parent | ☐ Legal Guardian | ☐ Other (Specify)

Understanding a W-2 form

READ THE TAX FORM

A W-2 form tells you how much money you made last year.
It also tells you the taxes you paid. Workers get these forms
in January. Read the form and answer the questions.

Employer's identification number 06-33231687		Wages, tips, other compensation $25,570.00	Federal income tax withheld $3,068.40
Employer's name , address, and zip code		Social Security Wages $25,570.00	Social Security tax withheld $1,534.20
Paco's Restaurant 1140 First Street San Jose, CA 95128		Medicare wages and tips $25,570.00	Medicare tax withheld $383.55
Employee's Social Security number 000-01-8243			
Employee's name , address, and zip code Rosa Encida 1245 Lane Street San Jose, CA 95128			

Name of State	State wages, tips, etc.	State income tax		
CA	$25,570.00	$2,045.60		

FORM W-2 Wages and Tax Statement 1999

1. Who does the form belong to? _____ Rosa Encida _____

2. Where does she work? _____

3. What year is this form for? _____

4. How much did she earn in 1999? _____

5. How much was her state income tax in 1999? _____

CultureNotes

At the end of each year, you get tax forms from your employer, your bank, and
the government. What do you do if you don't receive a tax form?

Performance Check How well can you use the skills in this unit?

Complete the activities. Go over your work with a partner or your teacher. Then complete the Performance Review on page 86.

SKILL 1   UNDERSTAND PAYCHECKS

Look at the paycheck. Circle the answer.

1. $70.20 is the: FICA   federal tax

2. $585 is the: gross pay   deductions

3. $500.80 is the: net pay   FICA

NO. 10000741

Albert Diego	111-22-3333			DEDUCTIONS	
RATE	HOURS	EARNINGS	YEAR TO DATE	Federal tax	$70.20
				FICA	12.00
$9.00	65.00	$585.00	$11,115.00	Medicare	2.00
				Total deductions	$84.20

GROSS PAY $585.00
PAY PERIOD BEGINNING   08/15/99
PAY PERIOD ENDING   09/01/99

NET PAY	$500.80

Park Auto Supply

Bank of Texas
Houston, Texas

NO. 10000741

PAY TO THE
ORDER OF   Albert Diego

DATE 09/01/99

SAMPLE

FIVE HUNDRED DOLLARS AND EIGHTY CENTS

NOT GOOD AFTER 60 DAYS FROM DATE ISSUED
MUST BE COUNTERSIGNED OVER $5000.00

PAY THIS AMOUNT
****500.80

⑈200005413⑈ ⑆053107989⑆ 480026251⑈

SKILL 2   REPORT MISTAKES IN YOUR PAYCHECK

Usually you make $10 an hour, but this week your check is for $9 per hour. Imagine that your partner or teacher is your boss. Report the mistake.

Write *yes* or *no*.

1. Social Security helps only older people. _____

2. Deductions from workers' paychecks help pay for Social Security. _____

3. To work in the United States, you must pay Social Security taxes. _____

SKILL 4   **UNDERSTAND A W-2 FORM**

How much federal tax did Martin pay? Circle the amount.

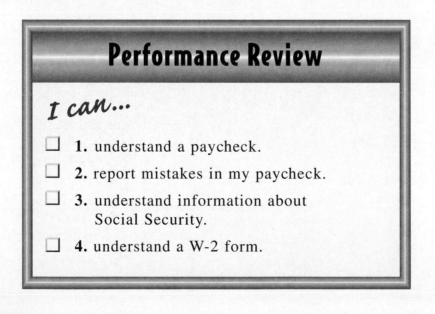

FORM **W-2** Wages and Tax Statement **1999**		Employee's Social Security number 000-64-7243	
Employer's name, address, and zip code Burger House 420 Forest Street Denver, Colorado 80223		Wages, tips, other compensation $21,300.00	Federal income tax withheld $2,556.00
			Social Security tax withheld $1,278.00
Employer's name, address, and zip code Martin Schenk 3245 Elm Street Denver, Colorado 80224			Medicare tax withheld $319.50
		State income tax $1,704.00	

Performance Review

I can...

☐ **1.** understand a paycheck.

☐ **2.** report mistakes in my paycheck.

☐ **3.** understand information about Social Security.

☐ **4.** understand a W-2 form.

DISCUSSION

Work with a team. How will your new skills help you? Make a list.
Share your list with the class.

Health and Safety

What do you think?

Where are the workers?

What safety steps are they taking?

What safety steps do you take at work?

Performance Preview

Can you...

☐ 1. understand safety instructions?

☐ 2. follow safety instructions?

☐ 3. complete an accident report?

☐ 4. report unsafe situations?

TEAM WORK

Look at the pictures. What health and safety equipment are the people wearing? Where do you think they work?

PARTNER WORK

Student A names a piece of safety equipment. Student B says what it is used for. Use the dialog and Useful Language.

A Safety glasses.

B Safety glasses protect your eyes.

 **SURVEY**

What health and safety equipment do you use at work? Ask your classmates. Make a chart. List the names of the equipment and why people use it.

Useful Language

safety glasses

back support belt

hard hat

boots

gloves

hairnet

dust mask

ear protection

 PRACTICE THE DIALOG

A It's really hot in here.

B I agree. We should ask for a fan.

A That's a good idea.

 PARTNER WORK

Talk about ways to stay safe and comfortable at work. Use the dialog and Useful Language above.

Useful Language

We should wear goggles.

We should sweep the floor.

We should put on gloves.

I think so, too.

I agree with you

TEAM WORK

Write some safety tips.

If you work in a hot area, you should use a fan.

ASAP PROJECT

Make a booklet of safety signs and rules. Include a list of the safety rules from everyone's workplace. Put in drawings of safety signs. Write what the signs mean. Complete this project as you work through this unit.

Keep Talking

Reporting unsafe situations

Look at the picture. Talk about the unsafe situations.

 PRACTICE THE DIALOG

Warn the people in the picture about the unsafe situations. Use the dialog below.

A Excuse me. There's broken glass on the counter. You should clean it up.

B You're right. Thanks for telling me.

Useful Language

If you sit like that, you could fall.

A cord is across the door.

You should put up a wet floor sign.

Personal Dictionary ▷ Keeping Safe at Work

Write the words and phrases that you need to know.

_____

_____

_____

Understanding safety instructions

LISTEN AND NUMBER

What are the people talking about? Write the number.

LISTEN AGAIN

What should the people do? Circle the letter.

1. **(a.)** Put the fan on the table.

    b. Turn off the fan.

3. **a.** Wear work boots.

    b. Wear work gloves.

5. **a.** Turn on the computer.

    b. Turn off the computer.

2. **a.** Set the brake on the wheelchair.

    b. Leave the wheelchair in the hall.

4. **a.** Put the mayonnaise in the refrigerator.

    b. Throw the mayonnaise away.

LISTEN AND CIRCLE

What should the employees do? Circle the letters.

a. wear hairnets

(b.) wear gloves

c. wear safety shoes

d. wear ear protection

e. wear safety glasses

f. wear a hard hat

g. wear aprons

h. wash their hands

Unit 8

A. Study the examples

You	should	wear long sleeves.
	shouldn't	

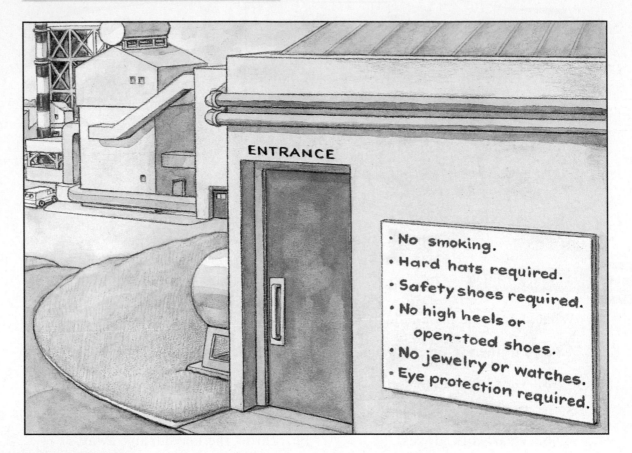

ENTRANCE

- No smoking.
- Hard hats required.
- Safety shoes required.
- No high heels or open-toed shoes.
- No jewelry or watches.
- Eye protection required.

SAFETY STEPS

Look at the picture. Write *should* or *shouldn't*.

1. Employees ____should____ wear safety shoes.

2. Employees _____ wear hard hats.

3. Employees _____ wear jewelry.

4. Employees _____ wear safety glasses.

5. Employees _____ smoke.

6. Employees _____ wear watches.

7. Employees _____ wear high heels.

Unit 8

B. Study the Examples

> If she goes into the factory, she should wear a hard hat.
> She should wear a hard hat if she goes into the factory.

TEAM WORK

Look at the picture on page 92 and then look at the picture below. Talk about what the woman should and shouldn't do if she goes into the factory.

COMPLETE THE SENTENCES

Write the letter of the answer.

1. If you work around food, ___c___ .

2. If you work on a construction site, _____ .

3. If you lift heavy boxes, _____ .

4. If you work at a gas station, _____ .

5. If you work around loud machines, _____ .

a. you should wear a hard hat

b. you shouldn't smoke

~~c.~~ you should wash your hands often

d. you should wear ear protection

e. you shouldn't lift with straight knees

TEAM WORK

What should you do at your workplace? Tell your team.

If you're a meat cutter, you should wear gloves.

READ THE SAFETY INSTRUCTIONS

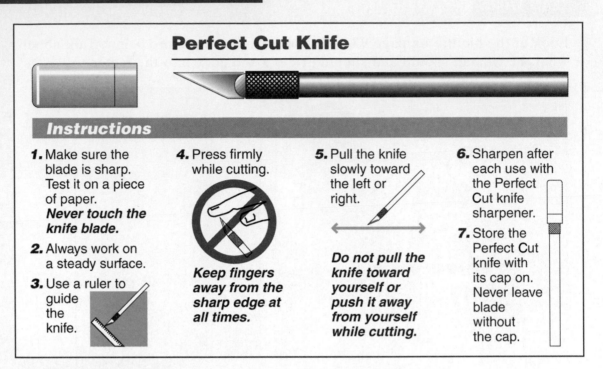

Perfect Cut Knife

Instructions

1. Make sure the blade is sharp. Test it on a piece of paper. ***Never touch the knife blade.***

2. Always work on a steady surface.

3. Use a ruler to guide the knife.

4. Press firmly while cutting.

Keep fingers away from the sharp edge at all times.

5. Pull the knife slowly toward the left or right.

Do not pull the knife toward yourself or push it away from yourself while cutting.

6. Sharpen after each use with the Perfect Cut knife sharpener.

7. Store the Perfect Cut knife with its cap on. Never leave blade without the cap.

SAFE OR DANGEROUS?

Is it safe? Write *yes* or *no*.

1. Test the blade on a piece of paper. __yes__

2. Touch your finger with the blade to test for sharpness. _____

3. Pull the knife towards yourself. _____

4. Work on a smooth, strong table. _____

5. Keep the blade sharp. _____

6. Store the knife with its cap off. _____

Tip Always read the instructions first.

Discussion

Is reading the instructions important? Many people do not read the instructions. Why don't people read instructions?

What happened to the man? How did he get hurt?

WRITE

Complete the accident report.

~~finger~~   hospital   supervisor   towel

The Frame Shop   *Accident Report*

Employee Name: **Carlos Salas**

Date: **December 15, 1999**

Description: **I was cutting. My _____finger_____ was over the edge of the ruler. I cut my finger. I wrapped my finger in a paper _____. I told my _____. She took me to the _____.**

 WRITE

Think about an accident you have heard about. Write a brief description for an accident report.

MATCH

Match the sign to the work situation.

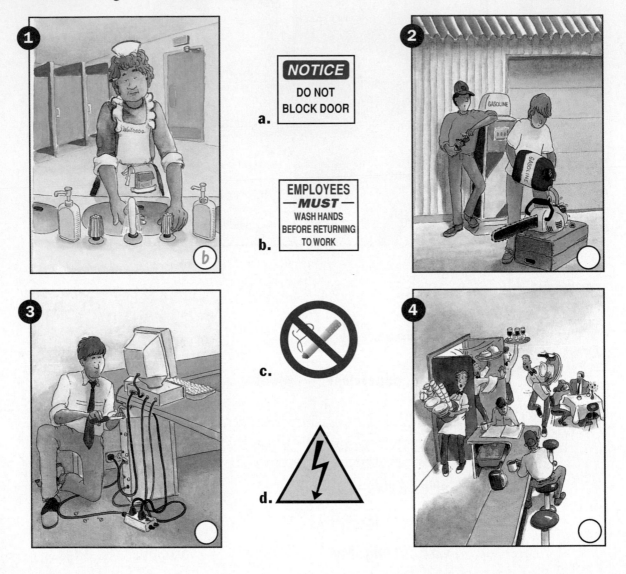

NOTICE
DO NOT
BLOCK DOOR
a.

EMPLOYEES
— *MUST* —
WASH HANDS
BEFORE RETURNING
TO WORK
b.

c.

d.

 *CultureNotes*

You see a situation at work that you think is not safe. What should you do?
How can you make your workplace safer?

Performance Check

Complete the activities. Go over your work with a partner or your teacher.
Then complete the Performance Review on page 98.

SKILL 1	UNDERSTAND SAFETY INSTRUCTIONS

Circle the safety steps you hear.

1. clean up the water   wear work boots   put up a sign

2. wear a hard hat   wear safety goggles   wear gloves

SKILL 2	FOLLOW SAFETY INSTRUCTIONS

Read the safety label. Circle the step that is not being followed.

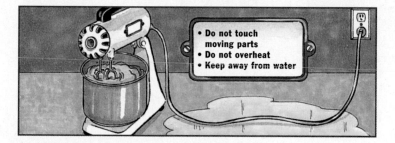

• Do not touch moving parts
• Do not overheat
• Keep away from water

SKILL 3	COMPLETE AN ACCIDENT REPORT

Imagine there was an accident at your workplace or school today.
Alice Witt slipped on a wet floor. She hurt her arm. She went
to the hospital. Complete the accident report. Use today's date.

Accident Report

Employee Name: _____

Date: _____

Description: _____

_____

What safety step should he take? Tell him. Circle the letter.

a. You should put on a hard hat.

b. You should put up a wet floor sign.

c. You should wear safety glasses.

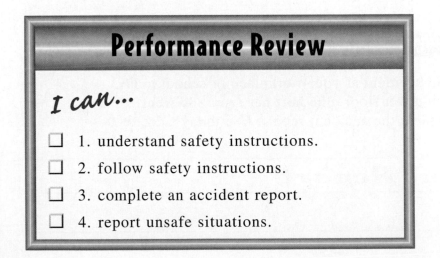

Performance Review

I can...

☐   1. understand safety instructions.

☐   2. follow safety instructions.

☐   3. complete an accident report.

☐   4. report unsafe situations.

DISCUSSION

Work with a team. How will your new skills help you?
Make a list. Share your list with the class.

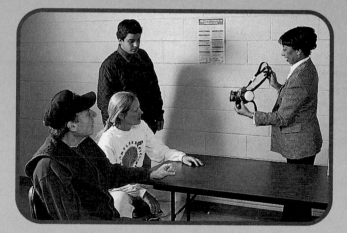

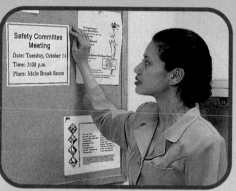

What Do You Think?

What are the people doing?

Do you have meetings at work or at school?

Who plans the meetings?

How do you participate in the meetings?

Performance Preview

Can you...

☐ 1. understand an agenda?

☐ 2. prepare for a meeting?

☐ 3. ask questions in a meeting?

☐ 4. make meetings work for you?

Getting Started

TEAM WORK

Look at the agendas. What information is usually in an agenda?

Data Input Department

Department Meeting Agenda

Topic: New Computers and Training

Date: 9/12

Time: 10:30 a.m. to 11:30 a.m.

Place: Meeting Room A

Purpose: To talk about problems with the new computers and set up a training schedule

10:30 – 10:35   Greetings and Introductions

10:35 – 10:45   Explain common problems with new computers

10:45 – 11:15   Discussion of our problems with the computers

11:15 – 11:30   Discuss needs for training

ALL EMPLOYEE MEETING

Tuesday

7:00 a.m.—8:00 a.m.

in the break room

Meet new employees — (5 minutes)

Stocking shelves — New procedure (15 minutes)

Pricing machines — Demonstration (15 minutes)

New food carts — (15 minutes)

Questions — (10 minutes)

PARTNER WORK

Look at the agendas. Ask and answer questions about the time, the place, and the topic of the meetings.

A   What's the topic of the first meeting?

B   New computers.

 SURVEY

How many students have been to a meeting at work? List the students' names. What were the meetings about? Make another list.

     Unit 9

 PRACTICE THE DIALOG

A Excuse me, Ms. Chen. Can we talk about Monday's meeting?

B Of course.

A Well, several people have questions about the new vacation policy.

B OK, I'll add it to the agenda. Thanks, Rhonda.

Useful Language

Could we discuss . . .

I'd like to talk about . . .

Could you give us more information about . . . ?

 PARTNER WORK

Your department is having a meeting next Tuesday. Your partner is the boss. You have questions about benefits, uniforms, or safety equipment. Suggest a meeting topic. Use the dialog and Useful Language above.

ASAP PROJECT

In teams, plan a meeting. Choose a topic you think is important. Decide who should be at the meeting. Choose a time and place for the meeting. Check that the place is open. Write an agenda for the meeting.

 PRACTICE THE DIALOG

A Excuse me. I'd like to ask a question.

B Go ahead.

A I have a question about our new dress code. Do we have to wear our company shirts every day?

B Yes, you have to wear the shirt and the pants every day.

Useful Language

I have a question.

Can I ask a question?

Is there time for a question?

 TEAM WORK

You're at a meeting. You have questions about the dress code, the attendance policy, or the benefits. Take turns asking your questions. Use the dialog and Useful Language above.

Personal Dictionary ▸ Meetings ·····

Write the words and phrases that you need to know.

_____

_____

_____

 **Listening**

 LISTEN AND CIRCLE

Circle the first speaker's topic.

1. (suitcases)   police

2. other hotels   hotel staff

3. how suitcases are stolen   police

4. hotel guests   taking suitcases off the bus

5. security guards   main entrance

LISTEN AGAIN

Circle the second speaker's topic.

1. police   (tour buses)

2. security guards   other hotels

3. how suitcases are stolen   police officers

4. bus drivers   traffic

5. police officers   security cameras

LISTEN ONCE MORE

Listen to the second speaker. Is the speaker polite or impolite?

1. polite   (impolite)

2. polite   impolite

3. polite   impolite

4. polite   impolite

5. polite   impolite

Grammar · Learning the language you need

A. Study the Examples

I We You They	have to go to a meeting.

He She	has to go to a meeting.

ANSWER THE QUESTION

Look at the supervisor's to-do list. What does the supervisor have to do? Write sentences using *has to*.

> ### TO DO
> Call the plant supervisors.
>
> Go to the main office.
>
> Call Mary in Human Resources.
>
> Send the package.

1. _____ He has to call the plant supervisors. _____

2. _____

3. _____

4. _____

 **WRITE**

What do the people have to do tomorrow? Write five sentences.

1. I _____ .

2. I _____ .

3. My boss _____ .

4. My coworkers _____ .

5. _____

Ask your partner what he or she has to do tomorrow.

B. Study the Examples

I'd He'd She'd We'd You'd They'd	like to ask about our vacation time.

 TEAM WORK

Talk about something you'd like to discuss in a meeting at your workplace or school.

A What would you like to discuss?

B I'd like to discuss the schedule.

A Good idea.

C. Study the Examples

We need to work faster because our customers want good service.
Our customers want good service, so we need to work faster.

MATCH

Match the need and the reason. Write the letter

1. We are having a meeting at work ___b___ .

2. I talked to my boss after the meeting _____ .

3. I want to get a good seat, _____ .

4. I'll take notes _____ .

a. so I'll arrive at the meeting early

b. because the company has a new uniform policy

c. because I had several questions

d. so I'll remember everything

Unit 9

Reading and Writing

READ THE AGENDA

✚ MERCY HOSPITAL MEMO

TO: All second–shift nurses and nursing aides
FROM: Head Nurse Marguerite Albats
DATE: June 1
RE: Meeting on June 14, 3:00–5:00 in the cafeteria

Here is the agenda for our next meeting. Please bring your ideas on these topics. If you'd like to add anything to the agenda, please let me know.

3:00 – 3:30   New equipment ◯

3:30 – 4:00   New procedures

         – Handling trash ①

         – Towel and blanket distribution ◯

4:00 – 4:45   Talk by Nurse Ryan: Dealing with Families ◯

4:45 – 5:00   Questions/Closing

READ AND WRITE

Frank made a list of questions for the meeting. When is a good time for him to ask each one? Write the number on the agenda.

1. What do we do with used needles?
2. How do we set the alarms on the new clocks?
3. What do we do about families that don't follow visitors' hours?
4. How do we keep track of extra blankets?

Many companies have agenda planners. Employees use them to plan meetings. Look at the meeting planner. What's the meeting about?

AGENDA PLANNER

Meeting Topic: <u>Problems with Customer Service</u>

Meeting Date: <u>January 27</u>

Topic: <u>Customers have to wait a long time to get service</u>

Topic: <u>We have to take inventory next week</u>

TEAM WORK

Your team is planning a meeting about learning English at work. Complete the agenda planner.

AGENDA PLANNER

Meeting Topic: _____

Meeting Date: _____

Topic: _____

Topic: _____

DISCUSSION

Share your agenda planner with the rest of the class. Compare agenda planners. Are there any changes you want to make?

Extension

Making meetings work for you

READ THE ARTICLE

Make Meetings Work for You

Most employees attend meetings from time to time. Follow these tips. See how you can make meetings work for you.

1. Get ready for the meeting. Find out the topic of the meeting, if possible. Read the agenda. Prepare questions.

2. Bring things you will need, such as a pencil, paper, and the agenda.

3. Be there on time or early. Sit where you can see and hear clearly.

4. Take notes. Write down important information.

5. Ask questions. If there isn't time, talk to the meeting leader or your boss after the meeting.

WHAT SHOULD THEY DO?

Write the tip number on the line.

1. Ed is at a meeting about quality assurance. There's a lot of

   important information he wants to remember. ___4___

2. Doris is going to a training meeting on new cash registers.

   She wants to be sure she can see the cash registers. _____

3. Clara is going to a meeting about benefits.

   She wants to find out about the dental plan. _____

4. Elena is at a meeting about the new attendance policy.

   She doesn't understand some of the information. _____

ON YOUR JOB *Culture Notes*

When you are in a meeting, it's important to show that you are listening. For example, look at the leader. Name more ways to show you are listening.

Unit 9

Complete the activities. Go over your work with a partner or your teacher. Then complete the Performance Review on page 110.

SKILL 1   UNDERSTAND AN AGENDA

Read the agenda. Write *yes* or *no*.

1. The meeting is about customer service. _____

2. The company is changing the telephone greeting. _____

3. The meeting is February 17. _____

CUSTOMER SERVICE DEPARTMENT

Employee Meeting

Agenda

Topic: Improving Customer Service
Date: February 16
Time: 3:00 p.m.
Place: Conference Room B

1. New telephone greeting
2. Expanded customer service hours
3. Responding to complaints

SKILL 2   PREPARE FOR A MEETING

What should you do to prepare for a meeting? Circle the numbers.

1. Read the agenda.

2. Tell everyone you don't like meetings.

3. Prepare questions.

4. Think of a reason to avoid the meeting.

5. Suggest topics to your boss.

Unit 9

ASK QUESTIONS IN A MEETING

You and your partner or teacher are having a meeting.
You have a question about uniforms, the schedule, or benefits.
Take turns asking a question politely.

SKILL 4 **MAKE MEETINGS WORK FOR YOU**

What should you do in a meeting? Write *yes* or *no*.

1. You should listen carefully. _____

2. You should finish other work during the meeting. _____

3. You should be on time. _____

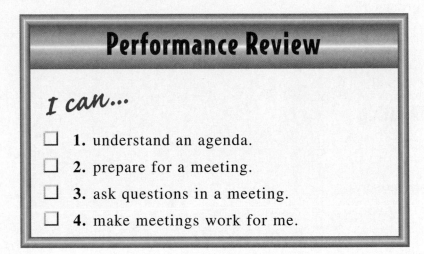

Performance Review

I can...

☐ 1. understand an agenda.

☐ 2. prepare for a meeting.

☐ 3. ask questions in a meeting.

☐ 4. make meetings work for me.

DISCUSSION

Work with a team. How will the skills help you? Make a list.
Share your list with the class.

What do you think?

Look at the pictures.

What are the people doing?

How did you find your job?

How did you apply?

Performance Preview

Can you...

☐ 1. look for a job?

☐ 2. interview for a job?

☐ 3. understand hiring decisions?

☐ 4. complete a job application?

Getting Started

TEAM WORK

Mario wants to look for a better job. To get ready, he wrote some notes about his education, employment record, and skills. What part of the job application does he write each fact on? Write the letter.

~~a.~~ I worked for Reliant Industries from 1997 to 1998.

b. I learned to install air conditioners at Fresh Air Cooling.

c. I studied English at Park Adult School.

d. I went to Rosario High School in Rosario, Mexico.

e. I work for Fresh Air Cooling now.

f. I have a commercial driver's license.

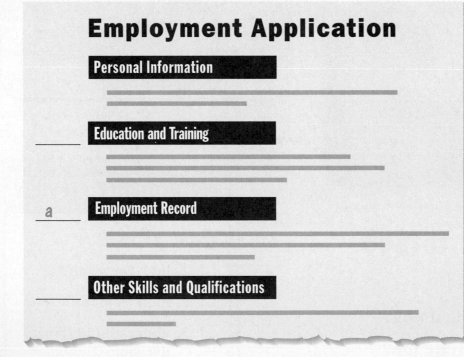

Employment Application

Personal Information

_____ **Education and Training**

a _____ **Employment Record**

_____ **Other Skills and Qualifications**

SURVEY

Make a list about yourself. Divide it into 3 sections: education and training, employment record, and other skills. Share it with a partner.
Add ideas to each other's lists.

Unit 10

Talk About It

Talking about work experience

 PRACTICE THE DIALOG

A Did you drive a van on your last job?

B Yes, I did. I drove a van part time for a florist.

A How long were you at that job?

B For three years.

A Why did you leave?

B I wanted full time work.

Useful Language

I was laid off.

I found a better job.

I wanted more responsibility.

 PARTNER WORK

Student A asks about work experience. Student B tells about his or her work experience. Use the dialog and the Useful Language above.

ASAP PROJECT

Work in teams. Think of different questions that interviewers ask. Make a list of questions about education and training, experience, work habits, and reasons for leaving a job. Copy the list and answer the questions. Use the questions and answers to prepare for job interviews.

Tip If you don't have specific job experience, talk about a related experience. If you don't have any related experience, say "I think I can learn that quickly" or "I'm a fast learner."

PRACTICE THE DIALOG

A Can you replace floor tiles?

B Yes, I have a lot of experience replacing floor tiles.

A Where did you learn?

B At Village Floor Company.

A Can you put down carpet?

B No, but I can learn quickly.

Useful Language

I went to City Technical School.

I got training on my last job.

My father taught me to put down carpet.

PARTNER WORK

Take turns interviewing each other for different jobs.
Use the dialog and the Useful Language above.

Personal Dictionary ▷ Getting a Job

Write the words and phrases that you need to know.

_____

_____

_____

Listening

LISTEN AND CIRCLE

Did they get the jobs? Circle *yes* or *no*.

1. (yes)   no   **2.** yes   no   **3.** yes   no

4. yes   no   **5.** yes   no

LISTEN AGAIN

Answer the questions. Circle the correct answer.

1. When can Ms. Binh start?

(in two weeks)   immediately

2. What are Eduardo's questions about?

hours and vacation time   pay and benefits

3. How did Sunja get the news about the job?

a letter   a telephone call

4. Who did Marta talk to?

Diego's teacher   Diego's boss

5. What position did Hermenia apply for?

secretary   marketing director

 LISTEN ONCE MORE

Why did they get the job or not get the job? Circle the letter.

1. a. She needs more computer skills.

  b. Her skills are right for this job.

2. a. He has experience managing people.

  b. He can use a computer.

3. a. The company hired a person from inside the company.

  b. The company decided not to hire for this position now.

4. a. His math skills are strong.

  b. He got along well with others and was on time.

5. a. The company hired someone who had more experience.

  b. The company hired a person who speaks English and Spanish.

Unit 10   115

Grammar

A. Study the Examples

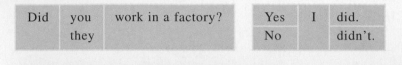

Did	you they	work in a factory?		Yes	I	did.
				No		didn't.

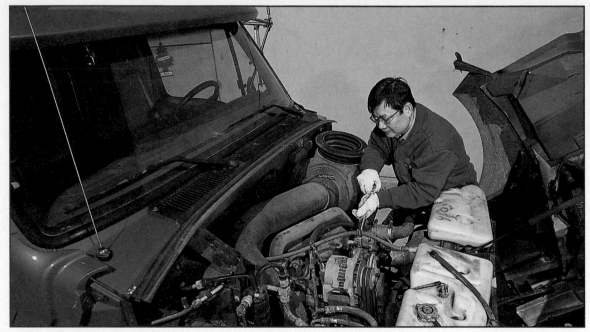

COMPLETE THE DIALOG

A _____Did_____ you _____work_____ (**work**) in a repair shop?

B Yes, I _____ . I _____ (**work**) in a repair shop
for five years.

A Did you _____ (**repair**) cars?

B No, I _____ . I _____ (**repair**) trucks.

A _____ you _____ (**study**) truck repair?

B Yes, I _____ . I _____ (**study**) for one year
at City Technical School.

A _____ you _____ (**show**) other workers how
to repair trucks?

B Yes, I _____ . I _____ (**help**) them with their work.

Unit 10

B. Study the Examples

I	drove	a van.
	didn't drive	

Irregular Verbs			
carry	carried	make	made
drive	drove	put	put
give	gave	run	ran
go	went	take	took
have	had	write	wrote

Tip Think about your past jobs before you go to an interview. Figure out positive things to say about each job.

COMPLETE THE SENTENCES

Use the language in B.

1. Bianca _____had_____ (**have**) a job interview yesterday.

2. He _____ (**not drive**) a taxi. He _____ (**drive**) a bus.

3. They _____ (**go**) to Gray Construction to find jobs.

4. Shirley _____ (**not take**) classes at Hall Technical School.

   She _____ (**take**) classes at City College.

5. Ron _____ (**make**) radios at Smith Electronics Company.

6. Eloise _____ (**put**) her name on the job application.

C. Study the Examples

I	learn quickly.
	answer politely.

Tip The words **hard** and **fast** do not add **-ly**.

She works fast.
He works hard.

COMPLETE THE SENTENCES

Use the language in C.

1. Nick does his work _____neatly_____ (**neat**).

2. He listens to instructions _____ (**careful**).

3. He doesn't work _____ (**slow**).

4. Nick teaches others _____ (**patient**).

5. Eva works _____ (**quick**).

Reading and Writing

READ

Figure out the abbreviations in the ads.
Write the abbreviations next to the words.

Assembly Positions
Avail. now. F/T, P/T. No
exp. nec. Will train.
$7.15-$8.60/hr. Apply
in person at Redwood
Creations, 110 Highway
12. No calls.

**Job Seekers
Wanted!**
The West Employment
Agency has been
placing qualified job
seekers for over twenty
years. Openings avail.
$6/hr. Assembly,
Packaging, plus many
more. Call today to set
up interview.
306-555-9000.

Child Care
City Nanny Service
seeks P/T child care
workers. Excl.
references req. $10/hr.
Apply in person,
35 Green St.

P/T Jobs/Bus Drivers
Excl. bnfts. $10/hr.
Req. 2 yrs. clean driving
record. P/T pos. avail.
Call 291-555-8163.

1. available _Avail._

2. experience _____

3. necessary _____

4. benefits _____

5. full time _____

6. part time _____

7. excellent _____

8. hour _____

9. position _____

10. required _____

ANSWER THE QUESTIONS

1. You want to apply for the bus driver job.
   What number do you call?   _291-555-8163_

2. You want a packaging position.
   Where do you apply?   _____

3. You want to interview at West Employment
   Agency. What number do you call?   _____

4. You are a child care worker. How much is
   City Nanny Service paying?   _____

DISCUSSION

How do you apply for each job? Which company do you call?
Which company do you visit?

Choose a job you'd like. Complete the job application.

APPLICATION FOR EMPLOYMENT

• PERSONAL INFORMATION

Name _____

Address _____

_____

Telephone _____ Social Security Number _____

Job Applied for _____

• WORK RECORD

Job Title _____ Company _____

Address _____

Telephone _____ How long were you at this job? _____

Job Title _____ Company _____

Address _____

Telephone _____ How long were you at this job? _____

• READ AND SIGN

The above information is true and correct.

Signature _____ Date _____

PARTNER WORK

Use your partner's application to interview your partner.

Unit 10

119

READ THE ARTICLE

Get the Job You Want!

Usually, the first time an employer sees you is at an interview. What can you do to look and sound right for the job? Here are some tips.

- Look your best. Make sure your clothes are clean and neat.
- Arrive 5 or 10 minutes early so the employer knows you can be on time.
- Bring a pen or a pencil with you so you can complete the application.
- Answer the employer's questions clearly. Talk about your experience. If you have no experience, say that you want to learn.
- Ask a few polite questions about the job.
- Don't smoke, chew gum, or drink coffee during the interview.

Remember, if you don't get the job, you are getting practice for your next interview. If you know how to interview, you can get the job you want.

WRITE

Write *yes* or *no*.

1. Look clean and neat for an interview. __yes__

2. It's OK to be late for an interview. _____

3. Drink coffee during an interview. _____

4. Don't ask any questions about the job. _____

5. Bring a pen or pencil with you. _____

 *Culture*Notes

How can you find out about job openings? Who can you talk to? Where can you look? Which ways are the most useful?

Complete the activities. Go over your work with a partner or your teacher. Then complete the Performance Review on page 122.

SKILL 1 **LOOK FOR A JOB**

Read the ad. Write the words next to their abbreviations.

Experience	full time	hour	required

Cook Needed.
Exp. req. F/T w/excl. bnfts.
Pay $9.40–$12.70/hr.,
based on exp. Call Carla
at City General Hospital,
555-4801.

1. Exp. _____

2. req. _____

3. F/T _____

4. hr. _____

What's the job for? How do you apply? Tell your partner or teacher.

SKILL 2 **INTERVIEW FOR A JOB**

Tell your teacher or your partner about your past work experience.

SKILL 3 **UNDERSTAND HIRING DECISIONS**

Listen. Check the reason the person did or didn't get the job.

1. _____ Another person had better computer skills.

_____ Another person had a commercial driver's license.

2. _____ Carolina can type and file papers.

_____ Carolina's interview was the best.

Unit 10

Fill out the application.

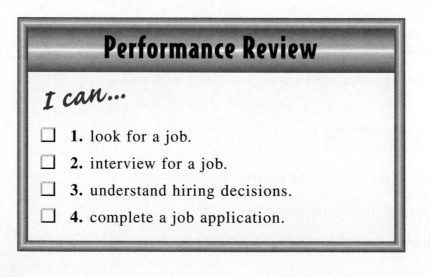

WORK EXPERIENCE

Job_____ Company _____

Address_____

Telephone_____ How long were you at this job?_____

Job_____ Company _____

Address_____

Telephone_____ How long were you at this job?_____

READ AND SIGN

The above information is true and correct.

Signature _____ Date _____

Performance Review

I can...

☐ **1.** look for a job.

☐ **2.** interview for a job.

☐ **3.** understand hiring decisions.

☐ **4.** complete a job application.

DISCUSSION

Work with a team. How will your new skills help you?
Make a list. Share your list with the class.

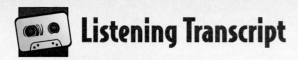

Listening Transcript

Listening (page 7)

LISTEN AND CIRCLE

Circle the name of the caller.

1.

A: This is Janie in the supply room. I can't answer the phone, but if you leave a message, I'll call you back.

B: Janie, this is Shelly in Accounting. I need two staplers. Please call me at extension 3317 and let me know if I can have them today.

2.

A: Big Mountain Skis. How may I help you?

B: I'm trying to reach Yolanda Marcos.

A: Yolanda's in a meeting. May I take a message?

B: Yes, will you please tell her that Mark at Computer Express called. The office computer is fixed and ready to be picked up.

A: Oh, good. She'll be glad to hear that the computer's fixed and ready. What's your number, Mark?

B: 555-9000.

A: 555-9000. Thank you.

3.

A: Spaghetti City.

B: Hello, is Sandra Lee in?

A: Sandra doesn't work on Thursdays, but she will be in tomorrow. Can I take a message?

B: Yes, please. My name is Young Kim. I'm calling about the waiter job.

A: Is there a telephone number where she can reach you, Mr. Kim?

B: Yes, it's 555-0191.

A: OK, then. I'll have Sandra call you when she gets back.

4.

A: Bright Industries.

B: I'd like to speak to Alice Wilson.

A: One moment. I'll transfer you.

C: Accounting.

B: Is Alice there?

C: Alice is away from her desk right now. Can I take a message?

B Yes, please. This is Winston Smith from Baker Office Furniture. Please tell Alice we will pay our invoice by Friday.

C: OK, Mr. Smith. I'll tell her that you will pay the invoice for Baker Office Furniture by Friday. Is there a phone number where she can reach you if she has any questions?

B: Yes, the number is 555-3200.

LISTEN AGAIN

Write the caller's telephone number or extension. *(Play the tape or read the transcript of Listen and Circle aloud again.)*

LISTEN ONCE MORE

Circle the reason for each call. *(Play the tape or read the transcript of Listen and Circle aloud again.)*

Performance Check (page 13)

SKILL 1   **TAKE TELEPHONE MESSAGES**

Listen to the telephone calls. Who's calling? Circle the letter.

1.

A: Sinclair Manufacturing. This is Isabel.

B: Good morning, Isabel. This is John Drummond.

A: Good morning, Mr. Drummond. How can I help you today?

B: I'd like to speak with Martin Valdez. Is he in?

A: I'm sorry, he's in a meeting all morning. May I take a message?

B: Tell him I called . . . and ask him to call back.

A: I'll give him the message.

2.

A: Good morning, Atlas Auto Parts.

B: This is Cindy Grey. May I speak to Ms. Mars?

A: Ms. Mars isn't available right now. Would you like to leave a message?

B: Yes, please. I have a 4:00 meeting with Ms. Mars today, but I'm afraid I need to cancel it.

A: All right, Ms. Grey. I will cancel that meeting for you. Would you like to reschedule?

B: Thank you, I would.

LISTEN AGAIN

What's the message? Circle the letter. *(Play the tape or read the transcript for Skill 1 aloud again.)*

U N I T ❷

Listening (page 19)

LISTEN AND MATCH

Match the item with its location.

1.

A: Welcome to the hotel, Lance.

B: Thanks.

A: You're going to need a uniform. Let's see . . . . What size shirt do you wear?

B: I usually wear a size medium shirt.

A: OK, let's go to the supply room and see if there are shirts your size in the closet. Otherwise we'll have to order them.

2.

A: I need Mrs. Anderson's file. She was here last in 1995.

B: After three years we put files in storage.

A: Can I still get to them?

B: Oh, yes. Old files are in boxes in the storage room. They're arranged by letter of the alphabet. They should be in a box marked A.

3.

A: What's the policy for people who forget or lose their room keys?

B: If they've got ID and sign this form with their name and room number, you can give them a spare key. We keep spare keys in a box in the security room. The keys are organized by room number, so they're easy to find. I'll show you the box when we go back to the security room.

4.

A: I'd like to touch up the paint around the new door in the maintenance barn. Where can I find the paint around here?

B: We keep paint in the storage room along with the cleaning supplies, extra furniture, and old computers. The paint is organized by date, so use the cans in the front first.

A: By date? What do you mean?

B: The cans of paint in the front of the storage room are older, and they're already open. We generally try to use them before we open new cans.

LISTEN AGAIN

Write the way the next item is organized. *(Play the tape or read the transcript of Listen and Match aloud again.)*

U N I T ❸

Listening (page 31)

LISTEN AND WRITE

Write the name of the machine on the maintenance report.

1.

A: Have you had a chance to check the microwave oven in the nurses' lounge yet?

B: Yes, I did. I changed the electrical cord. It was really worn.

2.

A: The lawn mower could use new blades, Ernesto.

B: I know, but there isn't any money in the budget to do that this month.

A: Well, I wouldn't worry too much. I just sharpened the blades. They should be fine for now.

3.

A: Hi, Morris. I saw you working on the van. What was the matter?

B: Nothing, really. I changed the oil. Otherwise everything looked OK.

4.

A: This cash register needed a key. What did you do?

B: I made a new key. I used the master key in the front office.

LISTEN AGAIN

On the maintenance report, write what each person did. *(Play the tape or read the transcript of Listen and Write aloud again.)*

U N I T ◆4◆

Listening (page 43)

LISTEN AND MATCH

What needs to be done in each meeting room? Write the letter next to the room.

1.

A: All right everybody, listen up. We have a busy day tomorrow and a lot to go over. First up, the Lake Room. Skill Seminars has an all-day meeting scheduled there tomorrow and they want 300 chairs set up. Chris, Manuel, Sandy, if the three of you work in the Lake Room, you should have no problem getting 300 chairs in there by 9:00.

2.

A: Next, Meeting Room 1. The Downtown Real Estate Association is having its monthly meeting in Meeting Room 1. They'll need the usual meeting table and ten chairs. Laura, can you take care of that by 8:30?

B: That was Meeting Room 1? They need a table and . . .

A: Ten chairs. By 8:30.

B: Got it.

3.

A: National Video Company is in Meeting Room 2 tomorrow. They need two long tables, 20 chairs, and a VCR. That room needs to be ready at 8:30, also. John, I'd like you to be responsible for Meeting Room 2.

B: Sorry, Tim. What was in Meeting Room 2?

A: Two tables, 20 chairs, and a VCR ready by 8:30. All right?

B: Sure thing.

4.

A: Finally, the Citywide Boy Scouts dinner is planned for the Grand Ballroom tomorrow night. They want us to set up for 600 people, so we're looking at 50 of the large round tables and 600 chairs. That all needs to be ready by 5:00, so I want all of you to move to the Grand Ballroom and start setting up in there as soon you're done with the other rooms. If we all work together on this, we can have those 50 tables and 600 chairs up in no time at all.

LISTEN AGAIN

Write the deadline for each task. *(Play the tape or read the transcript of Listen and Match aloud again.)*

LISTEN AND WRITE

When are the customers' appointments? Write the names on the schedule.

1.

A: Good morning. Lewis's Beauty Shop. This is Monica. How can I help you?

B: Monica, this is Ellen North. I'm calling to confirm my appointment with Lewis at 10:00 on Saturday.

A: I've got it right here, Ellen. Saturday at 10:00.

B: Thanks.

2.

A: Lewis's Beauty Shop. Lewis speaking.

B: Hi, Lewis. It's Hong. I was wondering if I could come in on Saturday for a haircut. I'm going on vacation and I could really use a cut.

A: Hi, Hong. I've got an opening at 11:00 on Saturday. Does 11:00 work for you?

B: That's great, Lewis. Thanks.

3.

A: Hello?

B: Hello, Mrs. Matesa. This is Monica from Lewis's Beauty Shop returning your call about your appointment with Lewis for Saturday at 9:00.

A: Hi, Monica. Thanks for calling back. I was wondering if you could change my appointment to some time later in the day.

B: I'm sorry, Mrs. Matesa. Lewis is booked all day. 9:00 is the only time he has open.

A: Well, OK. I'll see you then.

4.

Donna, this is Monica calling from Lewis's Beauty Shop. I'm calling to remind you about your appointment with Lewis for Saturday at 12:00. If you can't make it, please call and let me know. Our phone number is 555-3264. Otherwise, we look forward to seeing you Saturday at 12:00.

UNIT 5

Listening (page 55)

LISTEN AND CIRCLE

Where are the speakers?

1.

A: What's the special today?

B: That'd be the cheeseburger deluxe. It comes with fries and coleslaw.

A: Can I replace the coleslaw with a salad?

B: I'm sorry, but there are no substitutions on the special.

2.

A: May I help you?

B: Yes, I was wondering if I could get a refund on these clothes. I bought them here last month.

A: Last month? That could be a problem.

B: Why? I've got the receipt.

A: You see, we don't give refunds after ten days. But let me talk to my manager. She decides these things.

B: Thank you. Tell your manager I'd appreciate it if she could help.

3.

A: Is there a Speedy Mail store near the Town Hall?

B: Yes, sir. There's a Speedy Mail right on this bus route. It's one stop before the Town Hall. This bus stops right in front of the store. I'll let you know when we get there.

A: That would really help me out. Thank you.

4.

A: When will the tables be ready?

B: It should probably take us about a week to paint and assemble your tables. But don't worry. I know you need your furniture delivered on Saturday. We'll get it there in plenty of time. In fact, we'll make yours our first delivery on Saturday morning.

A: Thanks. I really need those tables no later than Saturday morning.

5.

A: Mr. Carlisle called to say he's coming back today to buy that stereo. He said he's looked at a lot of electronics stores and that we have the best prices in town.

B: Good, could you go down to storage and bring one up?

A: I already brought up the stereo he wants from storage. I put it behind the cash register.

LISTEN AGAIN

Match the request and the response. *(Play the tape or read the transcript of Listen and Circle aloud again.)*

Listening (page 67)

LISTEN AND CIRCLE

Listen and circle what the boss says during the performance review in column A.

1.

A: Dottie?

B: Yes, come in, Mary. You're here for your performance review, aren't you?

A: Yes, I am. Am I too early?

B: No, this is fine. It's always a pleasure to do your performance review. You're one of our best cashiers.

A: I like my job. I enjoy all the people.

B: It shows. You have such a good attitude. Your coworkers and managers all have nice things to say about you.

A: Well, it's easy to have a good attitude around here.

B: We've also noticed that you're very responsible. Your work area is always clean, and you're polite and helpful to your customers. And so, I'm pleased to tell you that you'll be getting a very nice raise this quarter. It will show up in your next paycheck.

2.

A: Lester, you're a careful worker, and that's important in your job. Your work is neat and well-organized.

B: Thank you, Lily. It's nice of you to say that.

A: There is one problem, however. You and I have talked about how important it is to get to work on time. But I notice that you're often late.

B: I know I'm late too much. Sometimes I'm late because I have to take my kids to school. But starting next week, my wife is going to take care of that.

A: That's good, Lester. I'm glad you're working on it. You really need to be here on time.

B: I will be.

A: In general, it's been a good year for you, Lester. But you have some things to learn and you need to work on your lateness, so I'm afraid there's no promotion this time around.

B: I understand why I'm not getting a promotion this year. But is there anything I should be doing so I can get one next year? Should I take classes or . . .

LISTEN AGAIN

What happens? Circle the answer in column B. *(Play the tape or read the transcript of Listen and Circle aloud again.)*

LISTEN AND CIRCLE

Circle all the reasons Sergio is Employee of the Year.

May I have your attention, please? As you know, every year at our annual picnic, I have the pleasure of announcing the Metro Bus Line Employee of the Year. This year's Employee of the Year award goes to the first assistant in our machine shop, Sergio Garcia.

Sergio's manager tells me that Sergio shows his commitment to his job in many ways. For example, he's never absent. Not absent once in five years. That's amazing. And his manager says that Sergio works hard and that he does good work. There's nothing more important than that in this or any other business.

To me, one of Sergio's best qualities is that he's a team player. He helps others whenever he can. His coworkers all know that if they have a problem, Sergio will help. And he'll help them in a friendly way, always with a smile on his face.

Many of you might not know this, but to be a good assistant, you have to think about the details. And Sergio thinks about the details a lot—he repairs and maintains our buses as if they were his own. And as president of Metro Bus Lines, that means a lot to me.

Sergio, would you please come up here and accept your award?

Listening Transcript

Listening (page 79)

LISTEN AND CIRCLE

What are the people asking about? Circle the letter.

1.

A: Stephanie, do you have a minute to answer a question about my paycheck?

B: Sure, let me take a look at it.

A: My paycheck shows my regular pay as $437.65.

B: Yes, I see that.

A: But I worked overtime last week.

B: Oh, overtime pay is added in separately because the pay rate is different. Here it is . . . your overtime pay for the paycheck is $92.50.

A: Thanks.

2.

A: My pay rate is $6.50 an hour, but on this week's paycheck it's $7.00. Do you know why?

B: I have a pretty good idea. Were you late any day this week?

A: No, I wasn't late at all.

B: Well then, that's why your pay rate is $7.00. It's company policy. If you're on time every day, your pay rate goes up $.50 an hour for the week.

A: I didn't know that. From now on I'll always be on time.

3.

A: Human Resources. This is Vivian.

B: Hi, Vivian. This is Bita Rami. I have a question about my paycheck.

A: Yes, Bita. How can I help you?

B: It looks as if the health insurance deduction wasn't taken out of my paycheck.

A: Was the deduction taken out of your last paycheck?

B: Yes, it was.

A: OK, tell you what. Bring your paycheck down to HR and I'll find out what happened to your health insurance deduction.

B: That'd be great. Thanks.

4.

A: Don, do you have a minute?

B: Sure, what's up?

A: Well, I think there's a mistake on my paycheck. Usually my federal tax is $48.50, but this week it's $78.00. Any idea why my federal tax would have gone up?

B: I can't imagine why that would have happened. I'll have to check with Human Resources on that one. I'll get right back to you.

A: Thanks, Don.

5.

A: Human Resources. This is Patty.

B: Hi, Patty. It's Christine.

A: Hi, Christine. What's up?

B: Well, I was out on Friday, so I didn't get my paycheck. Is it in your office?

A: Right. Your paycheck's here in Human Resources. When can you pick it up?

B: I can pick it up during my break.

A: See you then.

LISTEN AGAIN

Complete the explanation. Write the letter. *(Play the tape or read the transcript of Listen and Circle aloud again.)*

UNIT 8

Listening (page 91)

LISTEN AND NUMBER

What are the people talking about? Write the number of the conversation.

1.

A: Jake, that fan shouldn't be up there. Put the fan on the table.

B: It's not in anybody's way.

A: Last year a cook had her radio up there. It fell and splashed hot grease on her. She got burned.

B: Wow, I didn't think of that.

2. Set the brake on the wheelchair when you're not using it. It could roll away. Someone could get hurt.

3.

A: Mack, here's a pair of work gloves for you. Always wear them when you handle garbage.

B: How come?

A: Sometimes there are sharp things in the trash.

B: Will gloves really help?

A: These gloves will. They're pretty thick, and they have a special lining.

B: Thanks, I'll wear them.

4.

A: You should put the mayonnaise in the refrigerator after you use it.

B: But I'm going to use it again later.

A: Even so, it should go back in the refrigerator. If mayonnaise gets warm and spoils, it can make people sick.

B: Really? I didn't know that. I'll put it in the refrigerator.

5.

A: I finally figured out what's wrong with this computer. I just need to open it and fix one thing.

B: You really should turn the computer off before you open it.

A: I'm just going to do one thing.

B: It doesn't matter. When you work on the inside of a computer, you should turn it off first. You could easily get an electric shock.

LISTEN AGAIN

What should the people do? Circle the letter.
(Play the tape or read the transcript of Listen and Number aloud again.)

LISTEN AND CIRCLE

What should the employees do? Circle the letters.

Commercial Meat Cutting Company places great importance on employee safety. In fact, we have had over 1,000 operating days without a serious accident or injury. In order to keep up this record and stay safe, we follow these simple precautions.

First, we require everyone to wear gloves, safety glasses, and a hairnet. There are no exceptions. Managers and crew, employees, and visitors—everyone must wear gloves, safety glasses, and a hairnet. In addition, employees are expected to wash their hands regularly. They wash their hands before they begin work, before and after all breaks, and when they leave the plant at the end of their shift.

Performance Check (page 97)

SKILL 1 UNDERSTAND SAFETY INSTRUCTIONS

Circle the safety steps you hear.

1.

A: There's a lot of water on the floor by the door.

B: Yes, it's because of all that rain.

A: We'd better call maintenance. They can clean up the water and put up a sign.

B: Good idea. I'll ask for them to clean up the water and put up a sign as soon as possible.

2.

A: The new saw is really powerful.

B: Yes, you should wear safety goggles.

A: I've got goggles, but I think I need some gloves, too.

B: You're right. Make sure the gloves have a good grip.

UNIT 9

Listening (page 103)

LISTEN AND CIRCLE

Circle the first speaker's topic.

1.

A: As you all know, two suitcases were stolen from outside the hotel last Thursday . . . .

B: It's not our fault. We're really busy when the tour buses get to the hotel.

A: Please let me finish. We'll have time for discussion later. But you're right. When a tour bus parks in front of the hotel, there are many suitcases and many people on the sidewalk. However, it is still our job to be sure the suitcases are not stolen.

2.

A: Someone is taking suitcases from in front of other hotels, too.

B: Excuse me, James. May I add something here?

A: Yes, of course. You all know Morris Wright, manager of the bell staff.

B: Thank you. The other hotels do the same thing we do. The bus drivers take the suitcases from the bus and put them on the sidewalk. The suitcases are stolen from the sidewalk.

3.

A: We think that the person who is taking the suitcases works alone. He or she takes only one or two suitcases at a time.

B: Excuse me. Are you saying that a person just walks by, picks up a suitcase from the sidewalk, and walks away?

A: Yes, that's what we think happens.

4.

A: Here's an idea. Let's not leave the suitcases on the sidewalk. The bell staff could take the suitcases off the bus and carry them directly into the hotel.

B: What about the bus drivers? Couldn't they carry the suitcases into the hotel?

A: No, I don't think that would work. That's really not their job.

5.

A: We need to look at what the other hotels are doing. The Campbell Hotel hired security guards. The security guards stand on the sidewalk. They watch the buses, the people, and the suitcases.

B: James?

A: Yes, Natalie.

B: I heard that the Owens Inn uses security cameras to watch the tour buses. Are you thinking about installing cameras also?

LISTEN AGAIN

Circle the second speaker's topic. *(Play the tape or read the transcript of Listen and Circle aloud again.)*

LISTEN ONCE MORE

Listen to the second speaker. Is the speaker polite or impolite? *(Play the tape or read the transcript of Listen and Circle aloud again.)*

U N I T 10
Listening (page 115)

LISTEN AND CIRCLE

Did they get the jobs? Circle *yes* or *no*.

1.

A: Hello, Ms. Binh. This is Joyce from West Trucking.

B: Hi, Joyce. It's nice to hear from you.

A: We were very pleased with your application and would like to make you a job offer. The training you got at the Career and Technical Institute is excellent. Your skills are just right for the job.

B: I got the job? That's wonderful. Thank you.

A: You're welcome. We're very pleased, too. So tell me, when can you start?

B: How's two weeks from now?

A: Two weeks will be fine.

2.

A: Congratulations, Eduardo. With all your experience managing people, I think this will be a good job for you.

B: I think my experience managing people will be a help, too. That's one of the reasons I'm so pleased I got the job.

A: And you're ready to move to an office job?

B: Well, of course I'll miss being on the floor, but I think I can make a difference.

Listening Transcript

A: We do, too. Now let me take you down to Human Resources. They need you to sign some papers before you can get started.

B: Good. I'd also like to talk to someone there about benefits and pay. I have some questions.

A: I'm sure someone there can help you.

3.

A: Sunja, are you OK? You look a little sad.

B: I am a little. I just got this letter from Blue Star Industries.

A: Is it about the welder's job?

B: Yes, it is, and I didn't get the job.

A: Does the letter say why?

B: Let me read it to you. It says, "Thank you for coming to Blue Star to interview for the position of apprentice welder. However, we are not hiring for that position at this time."

A: So no one got the job?

B: I guess not.

4.

A: Hello, Diego. This is Marta Corona from Big Sam's Grocery. I'm calling to talk to you about the job as stock boy.

B: Yes?

A: Well, I talked to your teacher. She says you're a good student and a hard worker.

B: Thank you, Ms. Corona.

A: She also said that you got along well with your classmates and that you were always on time for class. So I think you'll fit in just fine at Big Sam's and I'd like to offer you the job. Congratulations.

B: I got the job! That's great.

5.

A: Marketing. This is Avis. How may I help you?

B: Avis, this is Hermenia Salvador. I interviewed for the secretary's job last week. I was wondering if I got the job.

A: I'm sorry, Hermenia. I was going to call you this afternoon. I'm afraid you didn't get the job. We hired someone who had more experience than you have.

B: I'm sorry, too. I really like your company a lot.

A: Look, after you finish your secretarial classes and have a little more experience, give me a call. Maybe we can work something out then.

B: Thank you. I'll do that.

LISTEN AGAIN

Answer the questions. Circle the correct answer. *(Play the tape or read the transcript of Listen and Circle aloud again.)*

LISTEN ONCE MORE

Why did they get the job or not get the job? Circle the letter. *(Play the tape or read the transcript of Listen and Circle aloud again.)*

Performance Check (page 121)

SKILL 3 **UNDERSTAND HIRING DECISIONS**

Listen. Check the reason the person did or didn't get the job.

1.

A: I'm sorry, Ted, but you didn't get the job. We hired someone who has better computer skills than you do. You have a lot of good experience, but you need to improve your skills on the computer.

B: I know I need to have better computer skills. That's why I've started taking classes at Norton Technical College.

A: That sounds like a good idea.

2.

A: Carolina, I've got some good news for you.

B: About the job?

A: Yes, that's right. You got the job. Congratulations.

B: Thank you.

A: I want you to know that we spoke with many people about the manager's job and that your interview was the best one. You spoke carefully and intelligently about your experience selling shoes and working with people. I think this is a great opportunity for you.

Listening Transcript

Vocabulary

**UNIT 1**

extension
message
Rolodex
telephone number
telephone roster

**UNIT 2**

bulletin board
cart
file cabinet
file folder
glue
hammer
hand truck
ladder
paper clip
pen
rubber bands
scissors
stapler

top shelf
middle shelf
bottom shelf

box of
roll of

**UNIT 3**

cash register
lawn mower
microwave oven
vacuum cleaner
van

cash register tape
gas
oil
sponge
tire

change
make
sharpen

break
leak
spill

maintenance department
maintenance request

out of order

**UNIT 4**

first shift
second shift

appointment
calendar
holiday schedule
schedule

first
second
then

**UNIT 5**

refund
return
store credit

request
suggestion

of course
no problem
sure

**UNIT 6**

compromise
get along
goal
mission statement
rule

**UNIT 7**

earnings
federal tax
gross pay
health insurance

life insurance
net pay
state tax

Social Security

paycheck
payday
pay rate

**UNIT 8**

back support belt
boots
dust mask
ear protection
gloves
hairnet
hard hat
safety glasses

**UNIT 9**

agenda
meeting

date
time
place
topic

UNIT 10

education
employment record
interview
personal information
training

part time
full time

available
benefits
excellent
experience
hour
necessary
position
required

Irregular Verbs

am, are, is	was, were	have	had
begin	began	keep	kept
break	broke	make	made
bring	brought	pay	paid
build	built	put	put
buy	bought	read	read
come	came	ride	rode
cut	cut	see	saw
do	did	sell	sold
drive	drove	send	sent
eat	ate	speak	spoke
feed	fed	spend	spent
feel	felt	sweep	swept
find	found	take	took
forget	forgot	tell	told
get	got	think	thought
give	gave	wear	wore
go	went	write	wrote